B S

D1346496

LIBRARY OF
MONEY AND BANKING HISTORY
HISTORY

CHRONICON - PRECIOSUM

CHRONICON - PRECIOSUM

OR

AN ACCOUNT

OF

ENGLISH GOLD AND SILVER MONEY

THE PRICE of CORN and other COMMODITIES

AND OF

Stipends, Salaries, Wages, Jointures, Portions,
Day-Labour, &c. IN ENGLAND

FOR

SIX HUNDRED YEARS LAST PAST

BY

BISHOP FLEETWOOD

[1745]

REPRINTS OF ECONOMIC CLASSICS

AUGUSTUS M. KELLEY · PUBLISHERS
NEW YORK 1969

First Edition 1707

New Edition 1745

(London: *Printed for* T. Osborne, *in Gray's Inn*, 1745)

Reprinted 1969 by

AUGUSTUS M. KELLEY · PUBLISHERS

NEW YORK NEW YORK 10010

SBN 678 00492 7

LIBRARY OF CONGRESS CATALOGUE CARD NUMBER

68-55711

PRINTED IN THE UNITED STATES OF AMERICA

by SENTRY PRESS, NEW YORK, N. Y. 10019

Chronicon Preciosum:

OR, AN

ACCOUNT

OF

ENGLISH GOLD and SILVER MONEY;

The Price of CORN and other COMMODITIES;

AND OF

Stipends, Salaries, Wages, Jointures, Portions, Day-labour, &c. in ENGLAND,

FOR

Six hundred Years last past:

SHEWING

From the *Decrease* of the Value of MONEY, and from the *Increase* of the Value of CORN and other COMMODITIES, *&c.*

THAT

A FELLOW, who has an Estate in Land of Inheritance, or a perpetual Pension of Five Pounds *per Annum,* may conscientiously keep his *Fellowship,* and ought not to be compelled to leave the same, tho' the Statutes of his College (founded between the Years 1440 and 1460) did then vacate his *Fellowship* on such Condition.

By BISHOP *FLEETWOOD.*

To which is added,

An HISTORICAL Account of COINS,

Illustrated with several Plates of Gold and Silver COINS.

LONDON:

Printed for T. OSBORNE, in *Gray's-Inn.*

M,DCC,XLV.

Bishop *FLEETWOOD*'s

PREFACE

TO THE

READER.

*W*HEN *I had set down, in* the first Chapter, *the Reason and Occasion of writing this little Book* ; and, in the following ones *had given the Proofs of my Determination* ; and, in the last, *had shewn the Use and Application of them, I thought I had made an End of my Business.*

But the Bookseller, *it seems, is of the Opinion, that I should not shew myself respectful enough to you, unless I introduced you, by the way of* Preface. *To comply, therefore, with his Desires, I must needs think of saying something, tho' it be but to discover some of the Imperfections of this Book.*

The Chapters then, of Money, *might have been much more compleat, by the Addition of* 5 *or* 6 Plates *of the several* Coins *we have had*

since

since the Conqueſt.* *Of the* Golden *Ones,* I
deſpair of ever ſeeing a Collection, *of any tolerable Antiquity; ſince they who are beſt, as* I
*hear, provided of theſe Treaſures, can riſe no
higher than* Edward III.† *And for my own
Part, I have never ſeen any one Piece, older
than* H. VI. *and that was, I believe, a* French
*one too: - And I am confident, that to a common
Curioſity, a Piece of* Gold, *older than the* laſt
Edward, *will appear a very great* Rarity. *And
yet, for full* Five Hundred *Years ſince the Conqueſt, one may well imagine, that moſt of the
great Payments muſt have been made in* Gold;
ſince (as I think, I have made appear) for 300
Years after that Time, there were no other Silver *Pieces coined, than* Pence, Half-Pence, *and*
Farthings: *and for* 150 *Years next after, there
were no other than a* Groat *and* Half Groat,
Henry VII. *being the firſt that ever coin'd a*
Shilling, *and that too at the latter End of his
Reign, and but a very few of them: So that
when you read (out of that Paſſage of* Gervaſe
of Tilbury, *cited at large by Mr.* Lowndes,‖
and whom I have, by Miſtake, in Page 56, *cited
as writing in the Time of* H. I. *inſtead of* H. II.)
ſub omnium Oculis effundit in Scaccario xxiiii
Solidos, quos de Acervo ſumptos prius ſigna-
verit. *And a little after,* Reliquos vero xxiiii
Solidos mittit in Loculum. *When, I ſay, you*
read

---

* This Imperfection is in this Edition ſupplied.

† Becauſe he was the firſt King of *England* that coined
Gold into Current Money. See the *Hiſtorical Account* at the
End of this *Chronicon.* ‖ In his Eſſay.

The PREFACE.

read these Passages, and others like them, in ancient Writers of the Englilh *Affairs, you are not to conclude that there was then any such Piece as a* Shilling *coined, no more than you would conclude there was such a Coin as a* Pound, *tho' you often meet with the word* Libra. *Upon the whole Matter, till about* 1544, *the* Silver *Money of* England *consisted of* Groats, Half-Groats, Pence, Half-Pence *(called, of old,* Mails) *and* Farthings: *In any, or all, of which Pieces, it must have been very troublesome to have paid* 5 *or* 10 *thousand* Pounds: *which makes it somewhat strange, that no more* Gold *of* Ancient Kings *should be preserved among us. But so, the* Antiquaries *tell us, it is with* Grecian *and with* Roman *Pieces, there being* 40 Medals *preserved, for one Piece of* Current Coin, *that we can be sure of. So that the best Reason, why we have so few old* Gold Coins *remaining with us, seems to be, because they were (as we call them)* Current, *i. e. they might be easily spent.*

But this, that has been said, makes it appear, that a small Plate *or two* would hold the Coins of* Silver, *of* 500 Years. *For the Coins of* W. Conq. W. II. H. I. Stephen, H. II. R. I. John, H. III. Ed. I. Ed. II. *were only* Pence, Half-Pence, *and* Farthings. *The Coins of* Ed. III. R. II. H. IV. H. V. H. VI. Ed. IV. R. III. *were only* Groats, Half-Groats, Pence, Half-Pence, *and* Farthings. H. VII. *(as is above-*
A 2 *said)*

---

* See the Plates at the End of this Edition.

The PREFACE.

said) added to this Number the Shilling, *which is, I believe, hard to meet with.* H. VIII. *added no new* Species, *but, in his later Life, debaſed all the old ones.* Edward VI. *debaſed them yet more, but in his laſt Year made great Amends, and added* Crowns, Half-Crowns, Six-Pences, *and* Three-Pences, *(ſo that I have miſtaken,* Page 33. *in ſaying* Three-pences *were firſt coined by* Q. Elizab.) *As to the Coins of the Princes following, they have been in almoſt every Bodies Hands; but yet the Memory of their* Weight, Finenesſs, *and* Compaſs, *ought to be preſerved to Poſterity, much better than 'tis like to be. And we ſee the Neceſſity of the* late new Coinage *hath almoſt obliterated the Names of* E. VI. Q. Mary I, Q. Eliz. Jac. I. *and* C. I. *already. So that an* 100 *Years hence, it will be hard to know, what Sort of Money was coined by Them; which would be great Pity, ſince they coined excellent Money, both for Weight and Finenesſs, which is both to the Advantage and Honour of a Nation. This Evil,*† *I once thought to have remedied; but the Trouble of procuring, rather than the Charge of cutting a ſingle Piece of each* Prince, *ſince the* Conqueſt, *was, I found, too great for ſuch a One as I am; and whoeʼver attempts it, muſt be obliged to abundance of curious Perſons, who have theſe Coins in their private Cabinets. And I here beſpeak their Favour, if I ſhould ever have Time and Power to undertake it.*

I have

---

† Is remedied in this Edition.

I have also, in the Second Chapter, *omitted all* Quarter-Pieces *of* Gold, *of whatever Denomination, becaufe they will be eafily known, by knowing* the whole: *as alfo the* 5 l. *and the* 2 l. Pieces *of* Gold *of* Ch. II. *and the* 3 l. Pieces *of* Ch. I. *and fome other fuch like, becaufe they rather feem to have been* Medals, *than* Current Coin.

As to the Chapter *of* Prices, *it will be in every Body's Power to make it more compleat, by reading the old* Computus's, *that he fhall chance to light upon, and inferting what he finds wanting, or differing from the* Accounts, *that I have given: but moft efpecially the Gentlemen of each* Univerfity *will have it in their Hands, to make what Amendments they fhall fee good, out of their old* Rolls *and* Burfars Accounts; *which I look upon as the moft fure Guides, in Enquiries of this Nature; becaufe our General Hiftories do moftly give us the Prices of Things, which are* extraordinary, *either for* Cheapnefs, *or for* Dearnefs; *whereas the* College-Accounts *deliver faithfully the ordinary and common Price of moft Commodities and Provifions.*

One Thing more I muft obferve to you; that the Nature of the Work obliged me, I thought, to fet down the Names of the Authors, *out of which I collected the Materials of this Book; as well to juftify myfelf, as that you may recur to the Originals, whenever you pleafe, in the particular Years;*

Years; *as also to avert*, *a little*, *that Scorn*, *with which some*, *in their supercilious Gravity*, *may pursue the Collectors of such light and trivial Matters*; *when they shall find*, *that no* English Historian, *of any tolerable Esteem among us*, *hath failed to make Observations of the like Nature*. *Nay*, *some considerable Ones have made it so much their Business*, *that they seldom conclude a* Year *without informing us*, *whether it were a* dear *or a* cheap *one*.

This Remark will also help to remove the Ostentation of much Reading, *because there is no need of reading an* Author *throughout*, *to find what I have here discovered*; *the Method of many of them making it easier to do so*, *by setting down (as I said) the Price of Corn, and other Provisions*, *at the End of every Year*. *But so far I must needs ostentate my Reading*, *as to assure you*, *that I have viewed with my own Eyes*, *and transcribed from all the* Originals, *whatever I have set down*; *even many Particulars*, *which I have been content to give you very often in honest Mr.* Stow's *English*.

But, *after all the Care I could take*, *I am sensible*, *there must needs be many Faults*, *and many Mistakes*, *in a Work of this Nature*; *and One I have already found*, *which I think myself obliged to retract*, *in this Place*, *because it is too late to do it in its proper One*; *and that is*, *a Censure I passed on Mr.* Speed's *giving us so many* Two-pences *and* Three-pences *of* Saxon Kings,

Kings, *and fome others, fince the* Conqueft. *I was led into it, (as others have been) by thinking he intended to mark* Two Pences *and* Three Pences *by the Figures of* 2 *and* 3, *which I am now fenfible he intended for another Purpofe. And therefore, as it would be an Error in any One, to think thofe Pieces were coin'd fo early, fo I muft needs acquit Mr.* Speed, *either of being in that Error himfelf, or of leading any others into it by Defign, altho' thofe Figures are placed over the Coins I there mention in* Page 34. *I have made fome fort of Amends, however, for thefe Errors, by taking more than ufual Care, that you fhould have as few* Errata's *of the* Printer, *as is poffible in a* Work *of this fort.*

THE

THE
CONTENTS.

Chronicon

Chronicon Preciosum:

OR, AN

ACCOUNT

OF

Englifh *Money, Corn,* &c.

CHAP. I.

The C A S E.

THE Statutes of a certain College (to the Obfervation of which, every one is fworn, when admitted Fellow) vacating a Fellowfhip, if the Fellow has an Eftate in *Land of Inheritance,* or a *perpetual Penfion,* of *Five Pounds per Annum,* I defire you would be pleafed, to give me your Anfwer to thefe following Queftions; when I have firft told you, that the College was founded between the Years 1440, and 1460.

I. Whe-

I. Whether He, who is possessed of an Estate, of that, or greater Value, may make it over *in trust* to his Friend, and then safely swear to the Observation of such Statute, amongst the rest?

II. Whether He, who has not an Estate of that Value, when admitted Fellow, may keep his Fellowship; tho' he *afterwards* come to an Estate of that, or much greater Value?

III. Whether He, who is actually possessed of an Estate, of *Six Pounds per Annum*, as Money and Things go *now*, may safely take that Oath, upon Presumption, that VI. *l.* now, is not worth what V *l.* was, when that Statute was made.

The Answer to your First Question may be easily had, by your asking yourself another, *viz.* Whether that Estate, tho' made over to another, be not still *your's*, as to the Profits of it, for the present, and as to the Disposal of it, for the future? If it be, How can you safely swear it is not your's, when you have it to all Intents and Purposes? A Man may have a legal Title to an Estate, and yet not be Possessor of it, nor receive any Fruits of it; he may be outed by Violence; it may be entirely mortgaged; or sequestred for Payment of Debts; and during such Violence, Mortgage, or Sequestration, he may safely swear, he is worth but so much as

he

he truly and indeed receives, and nothing more, let the Eftate be never fo great in itfelf. And fuch an Oath as your's has not Refpect to the *Title* alone, but to the *Title* with the *Profits* of an Eftate. And fince the making over your Eftate does not (nor do you intend it fhould) defeat you of either, How can you fave your Oath, by making over the Title of it, and that, it may be, only for the prefent? No Man, but He who has a mind to it, can be deceived by fuch Collufion. If an *Act of Parliament* fhould difcharge all Debtors, who would fwear they were not worth five Pounds, would you believe your Debtor an honeft Man, who fhould take fuch an Oath, when you knew he had an Eftate fufficient to difcharge his Obligations to you, but had made it over to another, only to defeat his Creditors? Affure yourfelf, fuch making over your Eftate, would not preferve you from the Guilt of Perjury, neither before God, nor good Men, tho' you would fwear true *according to the Letter*. We lately heard of a Man, who, to fave himfelf from paying a certain Sum, affefs'd by *Act of Parliament*, made over a great Treafure to his Neighbour (ignorant of the Matter) and locked him fafely up in his Clofet, till he came into the Court, and took his Oath he had not fo much Money in the World; and then came back, fet his Neighbour at Liberty, and took his Treafure again into his own Poffeffion. All who heard it, faid he was a *perjured Villain*, and tho' he had eluded the Law, yet he remain'd a Debtor to God's Juftice, which would certainly
find

find him out. This was the extremeſt Impudence that could be practiſed; but aſſure your ſelf, all Colluſions of this kind are as great Prophanations of an Oath as his was. They who make over the Titles of an Eſtate, and yet reſerve the Profits, are, in the ſight of God (as well as their own) as much Maſters of thoſe Eſtates, as if they had the *Titles* of them alſo in their Cabinets.

Your *Second* Queſtion ſeems to require more Pains to anſwer it, than the Firſt. But it only *ſeems ſo*, for there is, in Truth, but little Difficulty in it, if you conſider never ſo little the plain and viſible Intention of your Founder; which was, No-body worth five Pounds *per Annum* ſhould be Fellow of his College: Why elſe ſhould he require you to declare, under an Oath, you would obey that Statute? It is manifeſt, that if you had an Eſtate above that determined Value, you could not take that Oath; and, if you could not take that Oath, you could not be admitted Fellow. The having that Eſtate therefore muſt of neceſſity hinder you, by the Founder's viſible Intention, from being *admitted* Fellow; will not the ſame Intention therefore hinder you from *continuing* Fellow? I do not, however, directly charge with Perjury, ſuch Continuation, unleſs you deny, or do induſtriouſly conceal, your having ſuch an Eſtate; becauſe I am not ſure you are obliged (by Virtue of your general Oath) to vacate, of your own Accord, your Fellowſhip, but to ſubmit to the Directions or Injunctions of your lawful Superiors, and

and the Judges appointed in fuch Cafes. But yet I think it fuch a Violation of that Statute, as I would not counfel you to venture on. And, it may be, another Cafe, not fo much removed from this, may better clear up this Queftion. Suppofe it appeared to be the Purpofe of your Founder, that no married Man fhould be Fellow of his College, and that before Admiffion, every one were required to fwear he was not married; might one be married *after* fuch an Oath, and continue Fellow, honeftly, and with a good Confcience? I believe you will not think he might; but will rather conclude, that the Force of that Oath was, by the Founder, intended to fecure his main Purpofe, of having none but fingle Men Fellows of that Society; and that That Circumftance which would have *prevented* his Admiffion, would alfo, at any time after, *exclude* him. Thus, I believe, you would determine in any other's Cafe, and without any Bias on your Mind; and yet fuch Oath does not, in Terms, directly take in future Time; but only fays, *I am not married: I am not worth fo much,* &c.

Your *Third* and laft Queftion will coft me more Pains, and you more Patience, before we come to the Conclufion; if we can come to any fatisfactory one at laft. The Queftion would certainly need no Anfwer, if it were afked in grofs, *Whether he who has VI Pounds* per An. *may fafely fwear he has not V?* When a Pound is in both Places (and has been fo for more than 600 Years) XX *s.* But as you have qualified it, by

by diftinguifhing the Times, it will require
both a good Cafuift, and a pretty good Hiftorian, to anfwer it abfolutely, and to your Purpofe ; which is (as I take it) to know, of what
Value you may now hold an Eftate, with Safety
to your Confcience, which is charged with the
Obfervation of that Statute, which vacates the
Fellowfhip of One who has an Eftate of Inheritance, or a perpetual Penfion of C s. or V l.
per An. A better Cafuift, I own, you might
eafily have found. But, it may be, you could
not fo eafily have found One, who hath in his
Readings made more Obfervations on the Price
of Corn, and other Commodities, at different
Times, than I have done, as you will perceive
by reading this long Letter. So that, for aught
I know, my Diligence may make you Amends
for what Want of Judgment may be found in me.
And I do not fay this in Vanity and Oftentation
of my Labour, but becaufe without a good
Share of Knowledge in thefe Matters, the beft
Cafuift in the World can never anfwer your
Queftion fatisfactorily. And indeed, as the
World now goes, the greateft (tho' I will not
think the beft) Part of Readers will be rather
apt to defpife, than to commend the Pains that
are taken in making Collections of fo mean
Things, as the Price of Wheat, and Oats, of
Poultry, and fuch like Provifions : Tho' I hope,
before I have done, to fhew you, that the Obfervation of thefe little Things may be of good Ufe,
in the Confideration of great Affairs. And
when you fhall find, that many a fingle Line

of

of this Letter has coft me the looking over a
great Book, you will rather think fit to commend my Induftry, than to difparage fo many
good Authors, out of whom I have gathered
thefe Materials: At leaft, you will think I
wanted no Good-will to do you Service, who
have taken fuch Pains to fatisfy your Queftion,
that if any ancient *Greek* or *Latin* Writer had
taken the like, and left us fuch a Collection, you
would have had the *Salmafius's*, the *Grævius's*,
and the *Gronovii* almoft out of their Wits for
very Joy.   But I am now come to your Queftion, and muft premife, before I fpeak to it, that
whereas you fay your Statutes were made betwixt the Years 1440, and 1460, I muft, to
fave Labour, call this Space *the Reign of* H. VI.
tho' his Reign began 18 Years fooner.

I do affirm then, with the beft Judgment I
have, that I am ferioufly perfuaded, that, altho'
you are actually poffeffed of an Eftate of VI
Pounds *per An.* as Money and Things go *now*,
you may fafely take that Oath, upon Prefumption that VI *l. now*, is not worth what V *l.*
was *then*, when that Statute was firft made.
Becaufe whoever fwears, fwears to *Things* that
are fignified by Words, and not to *mere Words*.
When a Word fignifies the fame Thing *now* in
Effect, which it fignified 260 Years ago, then he
who fwears to *Words*, fwears to the Things they
fignify; but when different Things are fignified
by the fame Word, then he who knows *that*
Difference of Things, cannot help giving fuch
Word its proper and intended Signification.   A
Pound

Pound (for Inftance) will buy either more, or lefs Corn (take it which way you will) *now*, than it would in *H.* VI. Time. A *Pound* is therefore of more or lefs Value *now*, than it was *then*; and the *Value* of a *Pound* is truly a *Pound*, and not its mere *Name*. It is not therefore the fame Thing *now*, that it was in *H.* VI. Time.

I wifh, I confefs, with all my Heart, that all Oaths were fo contrived and fo worded, that they might be taken with the utmoft Plainnefs and Simplicity; and that no Room or Occafion could be left for any mental Refervation, or Exception in the Mind: But I think it can never be; almoft all Words are Equivocal: And it is impoffible to fix a determined Senfe on the Denominations of Coin, when all Things purchafeable with Money are fo changeable and uncertain. I do not mean, that a *Pound*, a *Mark*, and a *Shilling*, might not be always fix'd, fo as to fignify XX *s.* XIII *s.* IV *d.* and XII *d.* but that it never can be fo ordered, in this World, that a Man fhould always, 200 Years ago, and now, and 200 Years hence, purchafe the fame Quantity of Corn, the fame Number of Chickens, and as many Yards of Cloth, at one Time as another, with a *Pound*, a *Mark*, or a *Shilling*. And if this cannot be, then I maintain, that a *Pound*, a *Mark*, and a *Shilling*, is not *now* the fame Thing with a *Pound*, a *Mark*, and a *Shilling*, 200 Years ago. And therefore I may fafely take my Oath, that, altho' I am worth VI *l.* as Money and Things go now, yet I am not worth V *l.* as Money and Things went 260 Years

Years ago, in the Days of *H.* VI. And if it be said, that I muſt needs take the Words of my Oath in their *Plain, Literal,* and *Grammatical Senſe*; I anſwer, That ſo I muſt, wherever I can; but in this Caſe, the *Plain, Literal,* and *Grammatical* Senſe of *Five Pounds,* is not the ſame, with what it was 260 Years ago. What ſhall I do then? Shall I prefer the *Plain, Literal,* and *Grammatical* Senſe of Words at this preſent, before the *Plain, Literal,* and *Grammatical* Senſe of the ſame Words as it ſtood 260 Years ago; which, I am ſure, was the Senſe of the Founder? I grant, that if it were *a Caſe in Law,* I ſhould be determined by the Senſe which the Words do bear at preſent; but as it is *a Caſe of Conſcience,* I do roundly affirm, that V Pound is not the ſame Thing at preſent, that V *l.* was in the Reign of *H.* VI.

And that I may very honeſtly have Regard to the Value of V *l.* 260 Years ago, will, I believe, appear evident from what I am going to ſay; That the Founder intended the ſame Eaſe and Favour to Thoſe who ſhould live in his College 260 Years after his Deceaſe, as to Thoſe who lived in his own Time. Now, they who lived in his Time, might, with V Pounds, purchaſe ſo much Bread, ſo much Drink, Meat, Cloth, Firing, Books, and other Neceſſaries, or Conveniencies: I know not exactly how much, nor is it Material: I only ſay, the Founder intended I might keep ſuch an Eſtate, as would ſuffice to procure the ſame Bread, Drink, Meat, Cloth, Books, *&c.* as the other might have procured

cured for V Pounds, 260 Years ago. But this
I cannot poffibly do with VI Pounds, as Things
go *now*, nor it may be, with four times as much.
I may therefore have Regard (tho' in an Oath)
to the Value of *Pounds* at that Time; and, unlefs I have, I fhall be in a much harder Condition, than he, who lived fo long ago; which is
what the Founder neither did, nor could intend.
This Argument in general feems, to me, unan-
fwerable; and if you apply it to Particulars, you
will fee its Force more clearly. Ufe it, for Example, in the Bufinefs of *taking Degrees* in the
Univerfity, to which you know you are obliged,
and without which a Fellowfhip muft needs be
vacated. A *Degree* might be taken 260 Years
ago, at five times lefs Charge, than it can be at
this Day; and if a Fellow muft lofe his Fellowfhip for Want of a Degree, may it not very eafily
come to pafs, that he fhall not be able to pay for
that *Degree*, if he may not be worth more than
V Pounds *per An.* as Money goes *now?* Some
Founders have, in Cafes of extream Poverty,
made Allowances for indigent and virtuous
Scholars, towards the taking their Degrees: But
if you look into thofe Statutes, you will find that
thofe Allowances are (as Money and Degrees go
now) fo very inconfiderable, that they fignify
little or nothing towards it, which yet in thofe
early Days would (with a little Help of Friends)
have been fufficient to the intended Purpofe.
This is a clear Proof, that Regard both may and
muft be had, to the different Value of Money,
at different Times; and that the Founder's
visible

visible Intention is better answered by such Regard, than it would be by a strict and obstinate Adherence to the bare Letter of the Statute.

This Inconvenience (you may possibly object) will follow, from departing from the present Value of a *Pound*, and having Regard to what it was formerly; namely, That hereby too great a Liberty will be taken in Oaths of this Nature: Some will be apt to run the Matter too high, and (by reason of the Uncertainty we are in, what Proportion a *Pound* at present bears to a *Pound* in *H.* VI. Time) may pretend to keep their Fellowship, with an Estate of great Value. And to this I answer, That, for aught I know, it will now and then happen, as you surmise; nor is there any one Rule that is not subject to Abuse. And therefore I do not presume to set out, with any Exactness, or Certainty, and much less to determine Positively, how great an Estate is, at present, equivalent to an Estate, of the same Denomination 260 Years ago. I leave that to Others, to gather from the particular Accounts of Things that I shall give them, from our Historians. And they who are concern'd, ought seriously to consider, that altho' a *Pound* in *H.* VI. Time, might be worth 4 or 5, or more, in our own Times, yet it was not worth 20 or 30. And therefore the Uncertainty of its Value cannot encourage any reasonable Man, to advance it to an extravagant height. They who are the Guardians of your College-Statutes cannot (I believe) tell you exactly, how much
Land

Land of Inheritance, or how great a yearly *perpetual Pension*, will now-a-days anſwer to V *Pounds* in *H.* VI. Reign: but yet they can tell you that 60 or 70 *l. per An.* will be too much to keep together with a Fellowſhip, if it be *Land of Inheritance*, or a *perpetual Pension.* And furthermore (which is an Anſwer to all Objections of this Kind, and a ſufficient Reſtraint to all Exorbitance) theſe Guardians of your Statutes have it in their Power (if it be fit to have it in their Will) to judge according to the *Letter*, and to determine that V Pounds, as Pounds do *now* go, ſhall be the limited Sum, which ſhall not be exceeded. For the *Letter* is the Judge's Rule; and the Senſe he pleaſes to put on that *Letter*, is that by which you are to be determined, without Appeal or Remedy, unleſs he ſay that V *l.* is any thing leſs than an C *s.* And tho' I believe they never *will* determine, in any ſuch Caſe, without regard to Equity, and Reaſon, and comparing of Times, yet if they *ſhould*, you would be obliged to abide by their Judgment. And therefore all I have ſaid, or can ſay on this Head, is only to ſhew you, what I think may be ſafely done with reſpect to Equity, and a good Conſcience: Not to exempt you from the Juriſdiction of your lawful Superiours, but to ſhew you what you may do as an honeſt Man, tho' what you do, does not agree exactly with the *Letter* of the Statutes, to which you are obliged; nay (if you will) to ſhew you, what you may innocently do, even when you may be puniſhed for ſo doing.   But

But since I have said, that great Regard is to be had to the *Founder's Intention*, where, and as far as it appears; you may perhaps desire to know, from whence it comes to pass, that a Fellow is, without Dispute, allowed to enjoy the *Interest* of Money, or the Profits of a *Lease* to a much greater Value, than that of V Pounds *per An.* when the Intention of the Founder seems to be plainly defeated by so doing? I answer you, That the *Intention of the Founder* does not seem plainly to be defeated, by holding a *Lease*, or by receiving the *Interest* of Money; because of the *Uncertainty* of this Provision: Your Money may be lost by many Accidents; and if it should, then you are quite destitute, and undone: And a *Lease* is generally for a Term of Years, which you may chance to outlive, and then you may be in as ill a Condition: But *Land of Inheritance*, and a *perpetual Pension*, are as certain a Provision for Futurity, as the State of human Affairs will allow of. This, you see, makes a great Difference. But moreover, I do not say, that you are to seek for the *Founder's Intention* any farther than it plainly appears in his Statutes; nor that you are obliged, in many Cases, to argue from a *Parity of Reason*. Money was put out to *Interest*, and *Leases* were made, in the Time of *H.* VI. and your Founder, who lived in his Reign, knew this very well, and therefore had it in his Power to have mentioned, and excepted *Interest* and *Leases*, in his Statutes, had he so pleased; and not having made any such Exceptions,

Exceptions, you have no Reaſon to preſume, that his Intention was to except them, but to enjoy the Liberty he leaves you at. Where Law-givers are at Liberty to oblige and bind their Subjects, and may uſe what Terms and Words they pleaſe, to ſignify ſuch Obligation, their Words are preſumed to include no more than they expreſs: Their Silence neither profits nor hurts any one, 'tis their expreſs Words that do both.

Suppoſing, therefore, that you are convinced, that you may innocently ſwear to the Obſervation of the Statutes, and yet intend to keep your Fellowſhip, altho' you have an Eſtate of VI Pounds *per An.* upon Preſumption that VI. Pounds now-a-days, are not equal to V Pounds 260 Years ago.

Suppoſing, I ſay, this; I am now at Liberty to proceed to an Hiſtorical Account of Money, and of the different Price of Corn, and other Commodities; that by Underſtanding both, and Comparing one with the other, you may be the better able to determine what Proportion a *Pound*, a *Mark*, a *Shilling*, or a *Penny*, now, bears to the ſame Denominations many Years ago. For this Account of Money, you will be obliged to *Fabian*, and to *Stow*'s Chronicle, to Sir *H. Spelman*, and others, but eſpecially to Mr. *Lownden*'s *Eſſay*; I have only taken Leave and Pains to put Things into a Method which I thought better for my Purpoſe, and more for the Reader's Satisfaction, than any of theirs would be. And firſt, firft, of the feveral Names that you will often find in reading over our Hiftories, both *Latin* and *Englifh.* The *Gold* I have put *Alphabetically,* that Recourfe may be had more eafily to them; the *Silver,* as better known, I fpeak of gradually, beginning at the higheft, which is a *Pound,* and coming to a *Farthing,* which is the loweft Englifh Coin we have; and of which we have had none made of Silver (that I can find) fince the 36 *H.* VIII. *i. e.* fince 1542; and thofe were certainly very bad, fince out of 6 Ounces of fine Silver, (together with 6 Ounces of Allay) there were made 2304 Farthings, the Pound (as then moft abufively called) going at 48 *s.* All the Denominations of Gold were actually coined, at the Times I have fet down (and not fooner, that we can find.) But for the Silver, moft of them were mere Names, and were never coin'd; which they were, I obferve as I go along.

C H A P.

CHAP. II.

An Account of the Gold Coins.

ANGELS were doubtlefs fo called at firft, from an *Angel* impreffed on one Side of the Piece. And their Value was, at different Times:

			l.	s.	d.
Angels.	1	H. 6.	00	VI	VIII
	1	H. 8.	00	VII	VI
	34	H. 8.	00	VIII	00
	6	E. 6.	00	X	00
Half-Angels.	5	E. 4.	00	III	IV
	1	H. 8.	00	III	IX
	34	H. 8.	00	IV	00
	6	E. 6.	00	V	00

The Reader may perceive by this, that when he meets, in Hiftory, with the Word *Angels, Half-Angels, Farthing-Angels,* or with any other Coin, he muft obferve what King's Reign he is in, to underftand exactly what the Sum amounts to: for otherwife he will miftake. This I obferve to him, once for all, and go on.

			l.	s.	d.
Angelets.	1	H. 6.	00	III	IV
	34	H. 8.	00	IV	00
	6	E. 6.	00	V	00

From

From hence it appears that *Angelets* were the fame with *Half-Angels*.

		l.	*s.*	*d.*
Crowns of the Double Rofe.	I *H.* 8.	oo	v	oo
Britain Crowns.	I *Jac.* I.	oo	v	oo
	9 *Jac.* I.	oo	v	VI
Double Crowns.	I *Jac.* I.	oo	X	oo
	9 *Jac.* I.	oo	XI	oo
Thiſtle Crowns.	I *Jac.* I.	oo	IV	oo
	9 *Jac.* I.	oo	IV	IV *ob. q.*
Florens.	18 *E.* 3.	oo	VI	oo

They were fo called, becauſe firſt made by *Florentines*, as Mr. *Camden* fays. *Fabian* fays, that theſe were not of fo fine Gold as his *Nobles*, and *Half-Nobles* were. But that which is more obſervable is, that he calls the *Floren*, a *Penny*, value VI *s.* VIII *d.* The *Half-Floren* he calls a *Half-Penny*, value III *s.* IV *d.* The *Quarter-Floren* he calls a *Farthing*, val. I *s.* VIII *d.* And theſe Words you will often meet with, in old Hiſtories and Accompts, applied to feveral Coins, as *Rials*, *Angels* : Where you are to underſtand, by *Denarius*, the whole; by *Obolus*, the half; and by *Quadrans*, the fourth Part, or Farthing.

Thus, 1344, about this time, the *Noble*, *Obolus*, and *Farthing* of Gold, began to go about, faith *H. Knyton*.

		l.	*s.*	*d.*
Forty-Pence Pieces.	I *H.* 8.	oo	III	IV
Guineas.	22 *C.* 2.	o1	oo	oo *tho' they*

[*now paſs for* I *l.* I *s.*
Moton,

		l.	*s.*	*d.*
Moton, 1358, a *French* Piece of Gold, at	}	oo	ov	oo

Noble. So call'd, becaufe made of the nobleft and pureft Gold.

		l.	*s.*	*d.*
Noble.	18 *E.* 3.	oo	vi	viii
	5 *E.* 4.	oo	x	oo
	26 *Eliz.*	oo	xv	oo
George Nobles.	1 *H.* 8.	oo	vi	oo
Double Nobles.	26 *Eliz.*	oi	x	oo
Rials, or **Royals.** {	1 *H.* 6.	oo	x	oo
	1 *H.* 8.	oo	xi	iii
	2 *Eliz.*	oo	xv	oo
Rofe Rials.	3 *Jac.* 1.	oi	x	oo
Spur Rials.		oo	xv	oo

There is, in Dr. *Kennet*'s *Parochial Antiquities,* mention made of *Spurarium Aureum,* in *An.* 1292, or *Spur Royal;* but whether it were an *Englifh* Coin or not, does not appear.

		l.	*s.*	*d.*
Scute, a *French* Coin of Gold }	1427.	oo	iii	iv
Souvereigns.	1 *H.* 8.	oi	ii	vi
	34 *H.* 8.	oi	oo	oo
	4 *E.* 6.	oi	iv	oo
	6 *E.* 6.	oi	x	oo { *Old Stand.*
	——	oi	oo	oo 22 *Car.* [*fine.* 2 *Car. Allay.*
	2 *Eliz.*	*the fame in both Cafes.*		
Unites.	1 *Jac.* 1.	oi	oo	oo
	10 *Jac.* 1.	oi	ii	oo

Note,

Note, In 9 *Jac.* 1. by a Proclamation, Gold was raised 2 *s. per* Pound. *Ch.* the First brought it again to the Standard of 1 *Jac.* 1.

The following Table is collected out of Mr. *Lowndes's* Accounts, which, though they differ in some Points from Mr. *Stow's,* who also cites *Records* for some of them, I cannot chuse but prefer, because of his Abilities and Opportunities of giving them most perfect. Premising first, that a Pound of Gold, *Troy Weight,* was divided into 24 *Carats*; and each *Carat* into 4 *Grains:* And that the Old Standard of *England* was, 23 *Car.* 1. 3 *Grains* and a half of fine Gold, and half a *Grain* of Allay, which might be Silver or Copper.

	Fineness.	Allay.	Make in Silver.			
Years.	car.gr.	ca.gr.	l.	s.	d.	
18 E. 3.	23 3½	½	15	00	00	} The same
	23 3½	½	13	03	04	} Year.
20 E. 3.	23 3½	½	14	00	00	
27,30,37, 46 E. 3. 18 R. 2. 3 H. 4.	23 3½	½	15	00	00	
9 H. 5.	23 3½	½	16	13	04	
1 H. 6.	23 3½	½	22	10	00	
4 H. 6.	23 3½	½	16	13	04	
49* H. 6.	23 3½	½	22	10	00	
5 E. 4.	23 3½	½	22	10	00	

Fineness.

* It should be 39 *H.* 6.

Years.	Fineness		Allay ca.gr		l.	s.	d.	
8, 11, 16, 22 of E.4. / 1 R. 3. / 9 H. 7.	23	3½		½	22	10	00	
1 H. 8.	23	3½		½	27	00	00	} The same Year.
	22	00	2	0	25	02	06	
34 H. 8.	23	00	1	0	28	16	00	
36 H. 8.	22	00	2	0	30	00	00	
37 H. 8.	20	00	4	0	30	00	00	
1 E. 6.	20	00	4	0	30	00	00	
3 E. 6.	22	00	2	0	34	00	00	
4 E. 6.	23	3½	0	½	28	16	00	
6 E. 6.	23	3½	0	½	36	00	00	
6 E. 6.	22	00	2	0	33	00	00	
1 Mary	23	3½	0	½	36	00	00	
2 Eliz.	23	3½	0	½	36	00	00	
2 Eliz.	23	00	2	0	33	00	00	
19 Eliz.	23	3½	0	½	36	00	00	
43 Eliz.	23	3½	0	½	36	10	00	
43 Eliz.	22	00	2	0	33	10	00	
1 Jac. 1.	22	00	2	0	37	10	00	
3 Jac. 1.	23	3½	0	½	40	10	00	
10 Jac. 1.	23	3½	0	½	44	00	00	
10 Jac. 1.	22	00	2	0	40	18	04	
2 Car. 1.	23	3½	0	½	44	10	00	
2 Car. 1.	22	00	2	0	41	00	00	
12 Car. 2.	22	00	2	0	44	10	00	
1 Jac. 2 / W.& Mar. / Q. Anne.	22	00	2	0	44	10	00	

So

So that the fame Pound of Gold which in
18 *E.* 3. 1344, was worth 13, or 14, or 15
Pound in Silver, is rifen, by degrees, to go for
44 *l.* 10 *s.* and the Gold not quite fo fine neither. But if a Penny *then*, was worth our 3
Pence, and XX *s.* worth our LX *s.* then Gold
and Silver have kept, pretty near, the fame Proportion to each other; for three times 15 *l.* make
45 *l.* which is but X *s.* more than a Pound of
Gold now goes at.

C H A P. III.

An Account of Silver Money.

A Pound, *Libra*, contains 12 Ounces; and
tho' *now* it fignifies XX *s.* (when applied
to *Money*) which is but the 3d. Part of a Pound
in *Weight*, yet it is becaufe XX *s.* did heretofore weigh a full Pound, or 12 Ounces. Each
of thefe Ounces contained fo many *Solidi* or Shillings, and fo many *Denarii* or Pence, as they
who governed the Money-Matters thought fit;
fometimes more, and fometimes fewer. Dr.
Hicks, in his moft learned, ufeful, and labo-
rious Work (much to his own, and to the Nation's Honour) tells us, *pag.* 111. *Differt.
Epiftol.* that *the Saxon Pound contain'd LX
Shillings.* For this, he cites a Paffage out of
the

the *Textus Roffenfis*; *Ceorles Wergyld is Myrc-nalage CC Scill*. *Thegenes Wergyld is fix fwa micel*; *that byth XII hundred Scill*. *Thonne bith Cyninges anfeald Wergyld, fix Thegena Wergyld, be Myrcanalage; that is XXX thufend Sceata; that bith ealles CXX Punda*. The Englifh of which is, A Churle's Weregyld is, by Mercian-Law, 200 Shillings. A Thaine's Weregyld is fix times as much, *i. e.* 1200 *s*. And the King's fingle Were-gild is as much as the Weregyld of fix Thains; that is 30000 Sceata; which is in all 120 Pound.

The very fame Words we find at the End of King *Æthelftane*'s Laws, put out by Mr. *Lam-bard*; and afterwards by Mr. *Whelock* at *Cam-bridge*, 1644. *pag*. 56. excepting that it is faid here, that *a Ceorles Weregyld is* 266 *Thrimfæ, which make* 200 *Shillings*, and then goes on, as above; now if a Churle's Weregyld be 200 *s*. and a Thain's 1200 *s*. and a King's fix times as much, *i. e.* 7200 *s*. and this laft Sum make but CXX Pound, it will follow, that there muft go LX *s*. to the Pound, becaufe 120 multiplied by 60, produces 7200 *s*. But if, as it is here faid, 266 *Thrimfæ* make 200 Shillings, and (as is faid in the fame place, *pag*. 55.) that a King's Weregyld is among the Englifh 30 Thoufand *Thrimfæ*: then there will be found in 30000 *Thrimfæ*, juft 22400 *s*. and 208 *Thrimfæ* re-maining, which will make above 373 *l*. tho' you fhould allow 60 *s*. to the Pound; which is near to 3 times the Sum it ought to be. And if *Thrimfa* be (as that learned Perfon concludes) 4 *d*. of Saxon Money, then thirty thoufand
Thrimfæ

Thrimsæ will make 400 *l.* allowing 60 *s.* to each
Pound, which is more than 3 times 120 *l.* so
that nothing can be done with *Thrimsæ*, if 266
of them make 200 *s.*   Now if we will allow
but of a Miftake (not great in itfelf) of CXX
for CL, all things will go well, and the Saxon
Pound will continue, as it has all along been
counted, to be made up of 48 Shillings : for
150 multiplied by 48, makes juft 7200 *s.*
which is the King's *Weregyld.*   There is alfo
Reafon to believe, that in King *Cnute*'s Time
(who reign'd from 1017, to 1035,) the Saxon
Pound continued at 48 *s.* becaufe in his 3 *d.*
Law, it is faid, that he who breaks the King's
Peace in a *Head Church*, is to forfeit V *l.*   If
in a *Second Rate Church*, 120 *s.*   If in a *lefs
Church*, (but where there is a Church-Yard or
Burying-Place) 60 *s.*   If in a *Country Church
(Feld Cyric)* where there is no Church-Yard,
30 *s.*   Here you fee there is a gradual Diminution of the Mulct, V *l.* 120, 60, 30 *s.* from
whence I conclude that V *l.* was juft double
to 120 *s.* that is, it was 240 *s.* which will make
V *l.* at 48 *s.* the Pound ; and it will not be
double to 120 *s.* by any other Reckoning.   To
this, let me add, that Mr. *Camden*, Sir *H.
Spelman.* in his *Gloffary*, and Mr. *Lambard* in
his, do all of them agree, that the Saxon Pound
was made up of 48 *s.* and give no Intimation
that it was ever otherwife, either more or lefs.
I do not pretend, however, that Dr. *Hicks* has
not other Authorities, befides what is above-
cited, for what he affirms ; for he is fo well
skilled

skilled in these Matters, and has taken so much Pains in them, that he is not likely to say a Thing that seems so new, without good Reason. Let it then be said, that a Saxon Pound did *sometimes* contain LX *s.* but generally 48 *s.* and each Shilling contained 5 *d.* so that a Pound, or *Libra Anglo-Saxonica*, contained 240 *d.* How long it continued thus, I cannot tell exactly, but in the Laws, which are called King *Edward's*, 31. it is said, *In Denelega* : the Forfeiture for Breach of Peace, was VIII *l.* which was raised by the *Hundred.* Of this VIII *l.* the King received 100 *s.* the Sheriff 50 *s.* and the Bishop's *Decanus* (in whose Deanry the Peace was broken) the other 10 *s.* From whence it is clear, that VIII *l.* contained 160 *s.* which is 20 *s. per* Pound. But because 'tis manifest, from the 3d Law, that this Collection of *Edward's* Laws was made after *W. Rufus's* Time (since there is mention made of him, by Name, in it) it will be better to say, that the Pound contain'd XX *s.* in *William the Conqueror's* Time; because in the IVth of his Laws, *In Lege Danorum, foris factura est VIII lib. XX Solidi pro Capite, & VII libræ Regi.* In Danelagh, the Forfeiture is 8 *l.* 20 *s.* for the Head, and 7 *l.* for the King. And in 79 of *H.* 1. *Infractio Pacis Regis V lib. in Anglorum Lege. Media L* s. *& adhuc minoris, ubi parva Parochia est, & Atrium cum sit XXV* s. *& Campestris Capellæ, ubi non sit Atrium, XII* s. *VI* d. which is King *Cnute's* Law (above-recited) turn'd into *Latin*, and the Rates reduced to
the

the Money then current: which confirms my
Conjecture, that V *l.* was, *there,* double to
120 *s.* because it is *here* double to 50 *s.* And
whoever looks into the Laws of King *Ina, Alfred,* and others, and finds the same Propor-
tions of 120, 60, and 30 *s.* so oft observed in
the Fines or Forfeitures of Offenders, will be
apt to conclude that the Pound was then 48 *s.*

There is also some Dispute, whether the
Pound was made up of 12, or of 15 Ounces.
In the 30th of King *Ethelred's* Laws (as they
are in *J. Brompton)* you will find these Words;
*Let those who overlook the Ports, see, that every
Weight at the Market, be the Weight by which
my Money is received, and let each of them be
marked, so that* 15 *Oræ make a Pound.* And
in Sir *H. Spelman's Glossary,* you will find that
Ora signifies *Uncia,* and so in other learned
Authors. But the same most learned Knight
tells us, that *Ora* was also a Piece of Money,
valued at 16 *d.* for which he cites this Passage.
Plac. coram Rege T. Mich. 37 *H.* 3. *Rot.* 4.
The Men of Berkeholt, Com. Suffolc. *say, that in
the time of King* Henry, *the Grand Father of our
present Lord the King, they had a Custom that
when they would marry out their Daughters,
they were wont to pay, for Leave so to do,* 2
Oræ, *which are valued at* 32 d. Now 15 *Oræ*
make just a Saxon Pound, 48 *s.* or 15 times
16 *Oræ* make 240 *d.* There is therefore no
need of saying that *Ora* signifies an *Ounce* in
King *Ethelred's* Law, nor in the same Law re-
newed by King *Cnute,* (but which ought to
be

be corrected by the Law of *Ethelred*, for in-
stead of *ad Mercatum*, it is corruptly written
admetatum) Mr. *Somner* indeed [to whose
Judgment great regard is to be had in all these
Matters] is of the Opinion, that there was never any such Piece of Money as an *Ora*, but
that it always signifies an *Ounce*, of which he
says there were two sorts, the one containing
16 *Den.* the other 20, [of which there is so
frequent mention made in the *Dooms-day Book*]
which was called *the greater Ounce*. But then
he agrees that there were but 12 Ounces in the
Pound, which can hardly be reconciled to
Ethelred's Law. For if 15 *Oræ* are to make
a Pound, and *Ora* be an Ounce, there will unavoidably be 15 Ounces in the Pound. And
besides, he afterwards observes [from Mr. *Camden*, out of *Regiſtr. Burton*] that 20 *Oræ* are
said to be of equal Value with 2 *Marks* of Silver.
Now a *Mark* is 8 Ounces, [when XX s. make
a Pound in weight] and 2 *Marks* are 16 Ounces
[which he values at XXVI *s.* VIII *d.*] and if
20 *Oræ* be 20 Ounces [as they muſt, if *Ora*
be neceſſarily an Ounce] then 20 Ounces are
of equal Value with 16 Ounces; which may
be true of the *Pence* that are made of an Ounce,
but can hardly be true of the Name or Denomination of an Ounce. 12 Ounces, indeed,
of 20 *d.* are equal to 15 Ounces of 16 *d.* But
he who says that 12 Ounces are equal to 15
Ounces, muſt underſtand ſomething which his
Words do neither expreſs nor imply. It will
never therefore be true, that *Ora* ſhould always
ſignify

fignify an Ounce; that there fhould be 15 *Oræ*
in a Pound, and yet that there fhould be but
12 Ounces in the Pound. Whenever therefore
it is faid, that there are 12 *Oræ* in a Pound,
there Ora is 20 *d.* Whenever there are 15
Oræ in a Pound, then *Ora* is 16 *d.* *Verelius,*
in his *Lexicon Scandicum,* fays, *Ore, Solidus,*
& tertia pars Solidi. And *Dolmerus* (as he is
cited by *Du Frefne*) fays, *Ora, vernacula Aura,*
Danis Ore, fuit olim genus monetæ, valens 15
Minuta. Which would make one think it a
Denomination of *Money,* rather than of *Weight.*

It was a good Law of King *Edgar,* that
there fhould be the fame *Money,* the fame
Weight, and the fame *Meafures,* throughout
the Kingdom: but it was never well obferved.
What can be more vexatious and unprofitable,
both to Men of Reading and Practice, than to
find, that when they go out of one Country
into another, they muft learn a new Language,
or cannot buy or fell any Thing? An *Acre* is
not an *Acre*; nor a *Bufhel* a *Bufhel,* if you
travel but ten Miles. A *Pound* is not a *Pound,*
if you go from a *Goldfmith* to a *Grocer*; nor a
Gallon a *Gallon,* if you go from the *Alehoufe* to
the *Tavern.* What Purpofe does this Variety
ferve, or what Neceffity is there, which the
Difference of *Price* would not better anfwer
and fupply? 'Tis impoffible to fix the Price of
an *Acre* of Land, or of a *Quarter* of Wheat,
becaufe Land is much better in one Country
than another, and becaufe the Price of Corn
will depend upon the Plenty or the Scarcity of
it,

it, and that upon the Goodnefs or the Badnefs of the Soil and Seafons. But it is poffible to determine how many *Feet*, or *Yards*, Length and Breadth, an *Acre* fhall contain, in all Places alike; and poffible to determine how many *Quarts* a *Bufhel*, and how many *Bufhels* a *Quarter* fhall contain, fo that every Body fhall know thefe Things alike, and neither be miftaken nor impofed upon. Thefe things, I know, have (fome of them) been determin'd by Laws; but Cuftom and Folly have made thofe Laws ufelefs. And the Trouble that fuch Variety hath often given to me, as well as others, will juftify this Digreffion. From which I now return to fpeak of *Libra Anglo-Normanica*; which contained XX *s.* and each Shilling contain'd, fometimes 16 *d.* but generally 20 *d.* made out of an Ounce. The *Libra Denariorum*, and the *Libra Sterlingorum* are the fame; their Ounce containing 20 *d.* and in that they agree with the *Saxon* Pound, tho' they differ in the Number of Shillings. *M. Du Frefne* (not to be named without Honour) in *Libra Gallica*, fays, a Penny is the 20th Part of an Ounce; and that 12 *d.* make a Shilling, and 3 Ounces make 5 *s.* 'tis therefore the fame with *Libra Anglo-Normanica*. You will fee hereafter in the *Table*, how the Pound differed, by being divided into more or fewer Shillings. I need not obferve to you, I think, that there was never any coined Piece of Silver, that either weighed, or was called a *Pound.*

The

The next Denomination of Money, you
will often meet with, is a 𝕸𝖆𝖗𝖐, which the
Saxons call *Mancus, Mancusa, Mearc,* &c. and
amongſt them it came to XXX *d.* which was,
of their Money, VI *s.* Thus in the Laws of
H. 1. *c.* 35. it is ſaid, *XX Mancæ quæ faciunt
Solidos L.* Now you will wonder that 20
times 6 *s* (*i. e.* 120 *s.*) ſhould make but 50 *s.*
unleſs you remember that the 120 are *Anglo-
Saxonic* Shillings, and the 50 are *Anglo-Nor-
manic* ones, and that each of them contain
alike 600 Pence. Thus *c.* 69. *Debent reddi, ſe-
cundum Legem, XXX* s. *ad manbotam*; *idem
hodie quinque Marcæ.* Here both the XXX *s.*
and the *quinque Marcæ* are *Saxonic*; for there
are 5 times 6 in 30. And ſo again, *De Twelf-
hindo,* i. e. *Thaino,* 120 s. *qui faciunt* 20 *Mar-
cas.* In *c.* 34. *Erga Hundredum XXX* s. *&
V Denar. qui faciunt V Mancas, ut Solidus den.
XII. computetur.* Which brings the Mark to
VI *s.* 1 *d.* In *c.* 76. a *Mark* is but 4 *s.* 6 *d.*
but I doubt not but it is a Miſtake; and, indeed, thoſe Laws, as we have them now, are full
of Miſtakes: It is great pity Mr. *Somner*'s Cor-
rections, Annotations, and Gloſſary upon them,
are not publiſhed, but lie obſcurely in a private
Library: the Labours of ſo faithful and judi-
cious an Antiquary are well worth the Coſt that
any noble Lover of this ſort of Learning would
be at in making them publick, and would pay
him with ample Praiſe and Honour. When a
Mark came to be valued at XIII *s.* IV *d.* I cannot

not tell with any Exactneſs, but *M. Paris* in
the Life of *Guarinus Abb.* of St. *Albans*, in *An.*
1194, and in 1235, tells us that a *Mark* was
then (1194) 13 *s.* 4 *d.* and ſo it has continued to
this Day, without any Variation: how long before
that, appears not.　I muſt alſo obſerve here,
that there never was any ſuch Piece of *Silver*
as a *Mark* coin'd; and I cannot find any mention made of any ſuch Piece of *Gold*, ſince the
Norman Conqueſt; tho' probably there was, before, among the *Saxons*, with ſome Mark or
Signature upon it, for the Engliſh Word to
mark, does probably come from it, or that from
the Verb.

Angel: There was never any ſuch Piece of
Silver coined; but becauſe the Golden Piece of
that Name, was valued at X *s.* therefore X *s.* is
called an *Angel.*　And ſo it is with the Word

Noble. Which goes for VI *s.* VIII *d.* in Accounts: but there has not been any ſuch Piece
of Gold coined, at that Price, ſince the 9 *H.* 5.
and when they were firſt coined by *E.* 3. 1345,
they ſeem not to have been very acceptable to
the Nation, for thus *H. Knyton*, pag. 2484. re-
preſents the Matter.　*About this Time the Noble,
Obolus, and Ferthing of Gold, began to go about in
the Kingdom; upon which the Parliament ordained, that none of the Commons ſhould be compelled,
in any Payments, to take above XX s. of this new
Money.*　This was not, becauſe the Gold was
not good (for it was very fine, and of the *Old
Standard)* but becauſe, as I imagine, poor People
could

could not get it eafily changed into Silver, and fo
would be diftreffed; for at this Time there were
no Silver Coins, but *Pence*, and *Half-pence*, and
Qrs. it being, at the fooneft, 5 Years before there
were any *Groats* or *Half-Groats* coined: which
was about 1349. I fhall lofe half a dozen Lines
of my *Common-Place-Book*, if I may not under
this Head tell you, that in *An.* 1389, there
were feven Coiners condemned and hanged, for
bringing a *Noble* (not to 9 Pence, but) to X *s.*
making thence 6 *Quadrantes*, or Farthings. A
Noble of right contained 80 *d.* the *Obolus* or
Half contained 40 *d.* and the *Quadrans* or Farthing contained 20 *d.* But by thefe falfe Coiners,
a *Noble* was brought to 120 *d.* the *Obol.* to 60 *d.*
and the *Qu.* to 30 *d.* fo that there were 2 *Quadrantes*, above the 4 good ones; which was
their Profit. *Ed.* 4. raifed the *Noble* from VI *s.*
VIII *d.* to X *s.* which, tho' it was good Gold,
and called by another Name (a *Rial*) yet was
not well accepted, but thought to be to the Prejudice of the Commonwealth, but for what
Reafon I know not.

A **Crown.** The firft *Silver* Coin of the Va-
lue of V *s.* (that I can obferve) was in *Ed.* 6.
Days; the *Name* is old, but then it was always
Gold.

Half-Crowns. Of the fame Date with
Crowns, and never before.

Shillings, *Solidus.* The *Latin* Word is of
moft uncertain Signification, and to be determined by every particular Nation: but the Word
Scylling or *Shilling*, never fignified in *England*
but

but 5 Pence, with the *Saxons*, and 12 *d.* ever
fince: when it went for 12 *d.* at firft, is hard to
fay.   But, as common as this Word is, in all
Books, and all Accounts, yet there was never,
that appears, any Piece of Silver of that Denomination coined in *England* till the Year 1 504,
when *Fabian* fays, *A new Coin of Silver Groats,
and Half-Groats, and Shillings with half-faces,
was made.*   Stow fays, in the fame Year, *A new
Coin was by Parliament appointed,* i. e. *Groat
and Half-Groat, which bare but half-faces. The
fame Time alfo was coined a Groat, which was
in Value* 12d. *but of thefe but a few were coined.*
He does not call them *Shillings,* but *Fabian* does,
and he lived at that very Time, and was an obferving *Citizen.*   However, the Name does
not appear, in Mr. *Lowndes*'s Accounts, till a
great while after.   But *Stow* fays, 6 *E.* 6. *there
were coin'd, a Piece of Silver of V*s. *a 2d Piece
of II*s. *VI*d, *a third Piece of a Shilling*; *a 4th
VI*d. *and of fmaller Money, a Penny of the
Double Rofe, not Sterling but bafe; a Half-
Penny of the Single Rofe; and a Farthing with
a Portclofe.*   Alfo in 34 *H.* 8. there were coin'd
Teftons of 12 *d.* but not called *Shillings.* 13 *d.*
ob. 9 *d.* and 4 *d. ob.* were all Pieces that came
from *Scotland* in the Reign of *Jac.* 1. (tho'
fome of them were coin'd in *England)* and
therefore I meddle not with them.

    Teftons, Or, as we commonly call them,
Tefters, from a *Head* that was upon them,
were coin'd (as is before faid) 34 *H.* 8.   Sir
H. Spelman fays, they are a *French* Coin, of the
Value

Value of 18 *d.* and he does not know, but they might have gone for as much in *England.* He fays it was *Brafs*, and covered over with *Silver*, and went in *H.* 8th's Days for 12 *d.* but 1 *Ed.* 6. it was brought down to 9 *d.* and then to 6 *d.* (which ftill retains the Name) and in *An.* 1559 to 4 *d. ob.* *Stow* fays there was a fecond fort of *Teftons*, which in 1559 was cried down to 2 *d. q.* And a third fort that was made unpaffable at any Rate. 'Tis certain there were very good ones coined in *E.* 6th's Time; and they have ftill continued under all Princes, under the fame Name, and are the ufefulleft Pieces we have.

Groats. See of them, under a *Penny.* *Groffus* fignifies *great*; and a *Groat* was a *great* Piece with refpect to a *Penny*, which was but a 4th Part, and the greateft Piece (in all likelyhood) then coin'd.

Three-Pence. No mention made of them till 1561, when Queen *Elizabeth* coin'd them, with 6 *d.* 4 *d.* 2 *d.* 1 *d.* 1 *ob.* and *ob. q.* Pieces, and called-in all the bafe Money in the Kingdom; and fet our Coin upon that noble Foot on which it now ftands; which, becaufe it was of the greateft Benefit to the Nation, is one of the greateft Glories of her Reign; for thofe are the trueft and moft lafting Honours, that are built upon the Publick Good, procured or preferved by Princes.

Penny, *Denarius*, was the *firft* coined Piece of Silver we have notice of, and, for many Years, the *only* one; in *H.* 1ft's Days 'tis certain there

there were *Half-Pence*; and 9 *Ed.* 3. *cap.* 3.
'tis enacted, That no *Sterling*(*i. e.* Penny) *Half-
Penny*, nor *Farthing*, should be melted down
by the Goldsmiths; which is a good Proof,
that there were, at that time (which was *An.*
1335) no other Pieces of Silver coined. And
4 *H.* 4. it was enacted, That one *Third* of the
Silver coined, should be coined into Half-Pence
and Farthings. A *Penny* was indeed so much
the Whole of the current Coin of the Kingdom,
that *Denarius* was the same thing with *Nummus*, or Money: And therefore *Simeon Dunelm,*
1126, says, the Men that were found to have
made false *Money*, i. e. *Denarii* not of pure Silver,
were hanged. And (when it is any determined
Sum that is spoken of) *Nummus* does generally
signify a *Penny*. So *M. Westm. An.* 1095, says,
that tho' there were more than 300000 Men
marching to the *Holy Land*, yet Provision was
so plentiful that a *Ram* was sold at a *Penny
(uno Nummo)* and an *Ox* at (12 *Nummis*) 12 *d.*
Dr. *Hicks* (in his *Dissertatio Epistolaris*, p. 109.)
says, that the *Anglo-Saxons* had but *one* Silver
Coin among them, and that was a *Penny*. So
says Mr. *Camden*, Sir *H. Spelman*, and most of
our good Antiquaries. And therefore when
we find the honest and industrious Mr. *Speed,*
in his *Chronicle*, gives us the *Three-Pences* of
so many *Saxon Kings*, from *Cheuline* and *Egbert, An.* 562, down to *Ed. the Confessor*; the
Two-Pence of *Harold*; and again, the *Three-
Pences* of *W.* Con. *W.* 2. *H.* 1. *Stephen*, *H.* 2.
John, *H.* 3. and a *Two-Pence* of *R.* 1. and
that

that from the Treasury of that noble Antiquary Sir *R. Cotton*; we have Leave [for many Reasons] to think him mistaken; since in our Histories we find no Mention of any such Pieces as *Three-Pences*, before the Beginning of *Eliz.* The *Present State of* England (which is an excellent Book, and to whose Perfection every One should contribute, because it gives an Account of all our Affairs, both to Foreigners, and Natives) is also to be corrected in this Particular, when it says, that *in* Ed. *the* 1*st's Time* 4 d. 3 d. *and* 2 d. *were coin'd*, which certainly is not true. But all the Observations I shall make on the *Penny*, will be bestowed, in some few Notes, upon a Passage, which I have transcribed from Mr. *Stow* in the Year 1279, as follows.

‘ Whereas, before this Time, the Penny was ‘ wont to have a double Cross with a Crest, in ‘ such sort that the same might be easily broken ‘ in the midst, or into four Quarters, and so ‘ to be made into Half-pence, or Farthings; ‘ which Order was taken in the Year of Christ ‘ 1106, the 7 *H.* 1. It was now *(a)* ordained, ‘ that Pence, Half-Pence, and Farthings, ‘ should be made Round; whereupon were ‘ made these Verses following:

‘ Edward *did smite Round Penny, Half-* ‘ *Penny, Farthing,* ‘ *The Crosse passes the bond of all, throughout the Ring:*

‘ *The*

' The King's fide, was his head and his Name
  ' written (b)
' The Croffe fide, what City it was in coyned
  ' and fmitten.
' To Poor man, ne to Prieft, the Penny frayfes
  ' nothing,
' Men give God, ay, the leaft; they feaft him
  ' with a farthing.
' A thoufand, two hundred, fourfcore years
  ' and mo,
' On this Money men wondred, when it firft
  ' began to goe.

' And befides thefe Moneys, there was coined
' Groats (c) containing 4 d. the Piece (for what
' follows, he quotes Regiftr. of Bury) the
' Pound of Efterling Money, at this time, con-
' taining 12 Ounces; to wit, fine Silver (fuch
' as Men make into Foyle or Leaves, and is
' commonly called Silver of Gutherom Lane)
' 11 Ounces, 2 Efterlings (d) and one Ferling
' (e) and the other 17 d. ob. q. to be Allay.
' Alfo the Pound ought to weigh of Money
' XX s. and III d. by Accompt: fo that no
' Pound ought to be above 20 s. 4 d. nor lefs
' than 20 s. 2 d. by Accompt. The Ounce
' is to weigh 20 d. the Penny to weigh 24
' Grains (f).

Thus far Mr. Stow; to which let me add
to the Paffages that are mark'd, as follows.

(a) It fhould feem by thefe Words, that
Pence and Half-Pence were not Round, before

fore this Year 1279, but they were certainly *Round* in *H*. the 1ſt's Time. For in 1108,
Sim. Dunelm ſays, *the King appointed the Pence
and Half-Pence ſhould be all Round.* And in
1180, *Philip Aymary* of *Tours* was ſent for,
to new coin the Money; which was done, and
made all *Round*, as ſaith *Radulf de Diceto.* But,
it may be, that *Ed.* 1. was the firſt that appointed *Farthings* ſhould be coin'd (like *Pence*
and *Half-Pence) Round. Tho. Walſingham*
1280, and *H. Knyghton*, p. 2678, agree with
M. Weſtm. in 1279, to ſay the ſame thing;
that becauſe the Penny was broken in half, to
make 2 *Oboli*, and the *Oboli* again broken in
halves, to make 4 *Quadrantes* or Farthings, it
was ordained to coin the *Oboli*, and *Quadrantes*,
Round; ſo that the Opportunity of cutting
from each *Ob.* or *Quadr.* was taken away. And
yet the ſame *T. Walſingham*, in 1278, repre-
ſents Matters as if the *Obolus* had been diſtinct-
ly coined before this, in the Shape of a *Semi-
circle. Obolus qui prius formam habebat Semi-
circuli, tanquam pars Denarii in medio diviſi, fit
rotundus.* Whereas, in truth, whenever it
was in this Shape, it was certainly one half of
a *Penny*, broken in ſunder.

(b) Name written. The Name of the King
was indeed written, whether *Will. Henricus,
Ricardus*, or *Edvardus:* But no Body, from
thence, can tell whether it were *W*. I. or II.
Hen. I, II, III, IV, V, VI. or, *Ed.* I, II, III,
IV. and, as far as I could ever find, *H*. VII.
was the firſt that was to be certainly known
by

by that Diftinction, whofe Name I have feen
mark'd on a Silver Groat, *Henric*. VII. But
in this I may be miftaken, having not feen all
Coins, and yet enow to venture this Remark.

(c) **Groats.** This is the firft Time, that
I have feen *Groats* mentioned to be coin'd, in
1279. And tho' I never fufpect Mr. *Stow's*
Faithfulnefs, or Induftry, yet I believe he was
here miftaken; as well, becaufe in 9 *E*. 3. no
mention is made of them, when Pence and Half-
Pence are forbidden to be melted by the Goldfmith, fince the fame Reafon would have forbidden the melting down *Groats* (as afterwards
was done 17 *R*. 2.) which forbad the melting
the others; as alfo becaufe that Coin appears
not in Mr. *Lowndes's* Accounts, before the
27 *E*. 3. which was in 1353, tho' *Tho. Walfingham* mentions them in 1351, but he feems
not to have known there were ever any fuch
Pieces before that Year: For in that Year,
he fays, that, Wm. Edington, *Bp. of* Winton,
and L. *Treafurer, a Man of great Prudence,
but one who confulted more the King's Profit
than that of the Kingdom, found out and coin'd
new Pieces*; i. e. Groffum & dimidium Groffi.
*Groats and Half-Groats, but of lefs Weight than
they ought to have been. i. e.* I fuppofe, they
weighed not as much as 4 Penny's. After
this, we meet with the Name often, and moft
commonly applied to 4 *d*. tho' (as I think)
fometimes to more than 4 *d*. You may alfo
fee that 2 *d*. was not called by the Name *Two
Pence*, but a *Half-Groat*, or *Half-Groz*. And
in

in 19 *H.* 7. *Half-Groats* are called *Pence of Two-Pence.* *H. Knyton* mentions *Groffa* in 1378, and says it was 4 *d.* and so much was given to the King for every Man and Woman.

(d) Esterlings. Here *Sterling* signifies a *Penny-weight*, because it signifies a *Penny* of fine Silver, which is now called *Standard.* And I have never, but once, seen *Sterling* (when it signifies a Piece of Money) stand for any thing but a *Penny*, and that is, in *Monasticon Angl.* 2 Vol. p. 471. where it signifies a *Half-Penny:* For there it is said, that *Hens* were a *Sterling* a-piece; not in express Words, but by Consequence; for it is there said, that Wheat was 2 *s.* the Quarter; and that the 6th Part of a Bushel of Wheat was valued at a *Sterling*; now the Bushel is valued at 3 *d.* (when the Quarter is at 2 *s.*) and the 6th Part of 3 *d.* is a Half-Penny; and so *Sterling* must be there a *Half-Penny.* This was occasioned by *Ed.* 1. calling in *Pollards*, *Crocards*, or *Cocodones*, and *Rosary*'s; all which were coined, and brought into *England* by Foreigners, and underhand went for *Sterlings*, *(i. e.* for Pence,) but in the Year 1301, were suffered to go but for *Oboli*, or Half-Pence; and that not long neither: for at *Christmas* they were called in, and made *Oboli*; and at *Easter* following they were cried down quite: But Corruptions are not so easily parted with; they went current among the People longer, and retained still the Name of *Sterlings*, tho' they went for but *Half-Pence. H. Knyghton*, p. 2493.

(e) Ferling,

(e) Ferling, is a *Farthing*, or the 4th Part of a *Sterling*.

(f) The *Penny-weight* is here said to contain 24 Grains; and so it does to this Day. Yet *Tho. Rudborn, in Hist. Maj. Winton Anglia Sacra*, V. I. *p.* 257. says it was determined by *W.* Conq. 1083, that a *Penny Sterling*, round and unclip'd, was to weigh 32 Grains. However, we are sure it was so determined by Act of Parl. 51 *H.* 3. and so again, 12 *H.* 7. *That every Sterling shall weigh 32 Grains of Wheat, that grew in the midst of the Ear of Wheat; and a Standard for the King's Treasury is to be made according to this Assize.* To reconcile this Difference, 'tis probable, that 24 Grains, as they are Weights to weigh by, may be truly as heavy as 32 Grains of Wheat; which is as much as the Acts of Parliament require; and it would have been troublesome to have made a Brass Weight no heavier than the 32d Part of a Penny.

Obolus signifies an Half-Penny, or (as you have seen before) the half of any Thing. And as *Denariatus Terræ* signifies a *Perch* of Land (or let it be any other Measure, or Quantity) so *Obolatus Terræ* signifies *half* that Land; and a *Farthing* (called also *Fardella, Fardingdela, Farundel,* and other Names, which you may see in S. *H. Spelman's Gloss.)* signifies a *Quarter* of it. So *Acra*, an Acre of Land, contains (like a Mark in Money) 160 *Den.* 320 *Ob.* and 640 *Quadrantes.* I cannot find when *Obolus*, Half-Penny, was first coined: but

but we may imagine it was coined as early as ever we can find it mentioned, becaufe it is not a Denomination, which may be anfwered by other Money (as a *Pound* by 20 *s.* if there had been any Shillings, or a Mark, by 13 *s.* 4 *d.* or a Shilling by 12 Pence) but it muft be a diftinct coin'd Piece.   And fo for *Ferlingus*, or *Farthing*.   I fhall make an end when I have obferved to you, that when you meet, in old Donations, with fuch Words as *Librata Terræ*, *Marcata*, *Solidata*, or *Denariata*, and the like, you are to underftand as much Land as will yield the Rent of a *Pound*, a *Mark*, a *Shilling*, or a *Penny*, by the Year.

Here follows a TABLE, by which you will perceive into how many *Shillings* a Pound-weight of Silver has, at feveral Times, been coin'd ; together with its Allay, and what the Ounce was worth in common Eftimation.

Years.	Finen.	Allay.	Shillings.		Ounce worth.		
	oz.dw.	oz.dw.	s.	d.	l.	s.	d.
28 *E.* 1.	11 2	0 18	xx	iii	0	1	8¼
20 *E.* 3.	11 2	0 18	xxii	vi	0	1	10½
27 *E.* 3.	11 2	0 18	xxv		0	2	1
9 *H.* 5.	11 2	0 18	xxx		0	2	6
1 *H.* 6.	11 2	0 18	xxxvii	vi	0	3	1½
4 *H.* 6.	11 2	0 18	xxx		0	2	6
24 *H.* 6.	11 2	0 18	xxx		0	2	6

And thus it continued all the Reign of *E.* 3. *R.* 2 *H.* 4. till 9 *H.* 5.

Fabian

Fabian says, 23 *E.* 3. that he coin'd Groats and Half-Groats that wanted 2 *s.* 6 *d.* of the Old Standard, in a Pound *Troy.* This was in 1349, or 1350, but it is a Year, or two, too soon.

Years.	Finen.		Allay.		Shillings.		Ounce worth.			
	oz. dw.		oz. dw.		s.	d.	l.	s.	d.	
49 (39) H. 6.	11	2	0	18	XXXVII	VI	0	3	1½	
5, 8, 11,16, 24, {2. 4} 1 R. 3. 9 H. 7.	11	2	0	18	XXXVII	VI	0	3	1½	
1 H. 8.	11	2	0	18	XXXXV		0	3	9	
34 H. 8.	10	0	2	0	XXXXVIII		0	4	0	{In reality fine Silver 4s. 9d. ½ the Ounce.
36 H. 8.	6	0	6	0	XXXXVIII		0	4	0	In reality to 8s. the Oz.
37 H. 8.	4	0	8	0	XXXXVIII		0	4	0	In reality to 12s. the Oz.
1 E. 6.	4	0	8	0	XXXXVIII		0	4	0	In reality tp 12s. the Oz.
3 E. 6.	6	0	6	0	LXXII		0	6	0	In reality to 12s. the Oz.
5 E. 6.	3	0	9	0	LXXII		0	6	0	In reality to 1l. 4s. the Oz.
6 E. 6.	11	1	0	19	LX		0	5	0	
Q. Mary	11	0	1	0	LX		0	5	0	
2 Eliz.	11	2	0	18	LX		0	5	0	
19 Eliz.	11	2	0	18	LX		0	5	0	

Years.

Years.	Finen.	Allay.	Shillings.		Ounce worth.
	oz. dw.	oz. dw.	s.	d.	l. s. d.
43 *Eliz.*	11 2	0 18	LXII		0 5 2
Jac. 1.					
Car. 1.					
Car. 2.	11 2	0 18	LXII		0 5 2
Jac. 2.					
W. & *M.*					
Q. Anne.					

I cannot leave this Head, till I have taken
notice of one or two Specialties relating to Coin.
The firſt is, that when Sir *Rob. Cotton* was called to deliver his Opinion, touching the *Altera-
tion of the Coin,* before the Lords of the Privy-
Council in 2 *Car.* 1. he lays great load on the
Reign of *H.* 6. for Miſmanagement of this Affair of Money, as if it had ſuffered ſome extraordinary Debaſement in his Time, and
done him great Diſhonour, and great Miſchief
in the Minds of his Subjects, and afforded his
Rival (*Rich.* D. of *York*) an Occaſion of high
Complaint.   And that when my Lord Treaſurer *Burleigh,* and Sir *Thomas Smith,* were
called upon by Queen *Elizabeth,* to deliver their
Opinions about the Change of Money, they ad-
viſed her to reduce the Standard to the ancient
Parity

Parity and *Purity* of her Great-Grand-Father
King *Ed.* 4. Upon this, I cannot but obferve,
that *H.* 5. in the 9th of his Reign (according
to Mr. *Lowndes*'s *Accounts*) had raifed the
Money to XXX *s.* the Pound; and that *H.* 6.
in the firft of his Reign, advanced it to XXXVII *s.*
VI *d.* but keeping ftill to the *Old Standard* of
Finenefs (without a Change of which, all other
Changes feem to be but merely *nominal*; for 37 *s.*
and 6 *d.* will buy no more Wheat, than 30 *s.*
will do when once People come to know there
is no more fine Silver in 37 *s.* 6 *d.* than in 30 *s.*)
but even this Change continued not long, for
2 *H.* 6. *c.* 13. upon Complaint made in *Parliament*, that there was a Scarcity of *white Money*,
by reafon that Silver uncoined was bought and
fold at XXXII *s.* the *Pound Troy*; whereas it
was of no more Value, when coin'd, than
XXXII *s.* (12 *d.* abated for the Coinage) it was
enacted that none fhould buy or fell any Silver
uncoined for above XXX *s.* the *Pound Troy*,
befides the Fafhion. I will not anfwer for the
Reafonablenefs of this Act; but it proves clearly that the *Pound* did not long contain 37 *s.* 6 *d.*
and it appears evidently, that 4 *H.* 6. it came
again to XXX *s.* and fo continued to the very
laft Year of his Reign, when it was again advanced to 37 *s.* 6 *d.* and fo continued for near
50 Years. So that the greateft *Debafement* of
King *H.* 6. was juft equal to, and indeed the
fame with, the *Parity* and *Purity* of King
Ed. 4.

The

The greateſt *Debaſement* of Money, is the greateſt *Allay*, or Mixture of baſer Metal with Silver (and that is only bad, becauſe People are deceived by its Looks, and know not how much fine Silver there is in ſuch or ſuch a Piece) and that was in 5 *Ed.* 6. when 9 Ounces of *Allay* were added to 3 Ounces of *fine Silver*, and coin'd into 72 Shillings; ſo that a Pound of fine Silver, at that rate of Mixture, was coin'd into 288 *s.* or 14 *l.* 8 *s.* and the Ounce into 24 *s.* which was intolerable; and when in the Year following, this *Baſe* Money was called down, the People ſuffered extremely by it. I have by me now, an Account of that Time, wherein, by the *firſt* Proclamation (dated *July* 9.) a *College* loſt (out of an 118 *l.* 6 *s.* 11 *d.*) 29 *l.* 11 *s.* 8 *d. ob. q.* And by the *ſecond* Proclamation (dated *Aug.* 17. immediately following) out of 45 *l.* 3 *s.* the *College* loſt 15 *l.* 1 *s.* which was a 4th and a 3d Part of every One's Caſh, in the Space of two Months. It will be much for the Honour of *the late Reign*, to have remedied the greateſt Abuſe of Money, that was ever known in *England*, at a Time of the greateſt Danger and Expence, with very little Grievance of the People. But, ſure, 'tis better to prevent a moderate Miſchief, than redreſs a very great one; and, perhaps, a *Proclamation* of three or four Lines, forbidding any *clipped* Money to be received in the King's Exchequer, in 1690, would have prevented the clipping and ſpoiling 5 Millions. The *ſecond* Thing I would obſerve, is, That an Hiſtorian

rian who lived in the Days of *H.* 6. and *E.* 4.
tells us, that such was the Enmity of the *House
of York*, to *that of Lancaster*, that when *Ed.* 4.
came to the Crown, not only all that was
given and gotten, under the three foregoing
Reigns of *Henry* 4, 5, 6. was taken away;
but that the *Money* also, as well *Gold*, as *Silver*,
was changed and coined a-new, that the Name
of *Henry* might be no more remembred. *Sed
& Moneta tam in Auro, quam Argento, ut No-
men in ea prorsus deleatur* Henrici, *similiter mu-
tata est, & denuo fabricata. Continuatio Hist.
Croyland, An.* 1461. But Time hath made
all even again, and left us as many Coins of
the *Henry's*, as of *Edward* the 4th.

The last Thing I would observe to you is,
That tho' (as you see in the Table) the *Pound*
was sometimes 22 *s.* 6 *d.* 25 *s.* 30 *s.* 37 *s.* 6 *d.*
45 *s.* 48 *s.* 72 *s.* 60 *s.* and 62 *s.* as it now
stands : Yet, in *Accompts*, it always signified
20 *s.* just, and neither more nor less. When
the Pound contain'd (for Example) 30 *s.* he
who owed another Man *Five Pounds*, did not
pay him 150 *s.* but an 100. And 'tis as certain that an 100 *s.* signified *five Pounds* at that
time, and no less, as it does now. This must
have been ever since XX *s.* came to *weigh*, and
to be called, a *Pound*. And so it was with the
Saxon Pound, that was always 48 *s.* And he
who owed *five Pounds*, before the *Norman
Times*, did certainly pay 240 *s.* which was,
both in *Weight* and *Denomination*, five Pounds :
Whereas five Pounds are now only so in *Name*,
and

and not in *Weight*. Let me end this Chapter, with giving you the Names (from Mr. *Camden*) of feveral falfe and fmall Pieces, that were heretofore in ufe among our Fathers. In the Time of *E.* 3. *Crocards, Pollards, Rofaries, Cocodones, Stepings,* and *Staldings,* were cried down. *Gally-Half-Pence,* which were brought hither by the *Genoefe Gallies,* cried down by *H.* 4. *Sufkins* and *Dodkins* by *H.* 5. and *Blanks* by *H.* 6. There were alfo little Pieces coined by *H.* 7. called *Dandypratts,* which, I fuppofe, were little and contemptible Things, becaufe that Word has fince been ufed to fignify fmall and worthlefs People.

C H A P.

C H A P. IV.

Of the Price of Corn, *and other* Commodities, *for* 600 *Years laft paft.*

HAving difpatch'd, with what *Exaɛlnefs* I could, the Chapters of *Monies*, I am now come to fpeak to the Price of *Corn* and other *Commodities* ; which is (whether you know it or not) the readieft way to the Solution of your *Third*, and moft material Queftion. For, your Bufinefs is to know (as near as you can) what Eftate or Sum of Money will *now-a-days* be equal or equivalent to *five Pounds* (let that be the fuppofed Sum in this Difcourfe) in the Reign *H. VI.* and to this End, your Care will be, to find out how much *Meat*, *Drink*, or *Cloth*, might be pur-chafed in *H. VI.* Reign, with V *l.* and then to find out, how much of the Money now current, will be required to purchafe the fame Quantity of *Meat*, *Drink*, and *Cloth*. For, fince Money is of no other Ufe, than as it is the Thing with which we purchafe

the

theNeceffariesand Conveniencies of Life, 'tis evident, that if V *l.* in *H.* VI. Days, would purchafe 5 *Quarter of Wheat,* 4 *Hogsheads of Beer,* and 6 *Yards of Cloth,* he who then had 5 *l.* in his Pocket, was full as rich a Man as he who has now XX *l.* if with that XX *l.* he can purchafe no more *Wheat, Beer,* or *Cloth,* than the other. I do not mean hereby to pre-judge this to be the Proportion; but ufe this Inftance to let you fee, that this is the propereft way of coming to know, what Eftate is *now* moft anfwerable to an Eftate of V *l. per. An.* 250 Years ago. And tho' the comparing the Reign of *H.* VI. with your own Times, would be fufficient for your particular Purpofe; yet fince I have made the fame *Col-lections,* for the Years foregoing, and for thofe which follow the Reign of *H.* VI. it will be (I be-lieve) neither ungrateful nor un-profitable, to give them to the Reader; efpecially fince other *Colleges,* which may be under the like Obligations, were founded, fome *before,* and fome *fince,* the Reign of *H.* VI. It will be moft for the Reader's Ufe, and Eafe,

that

that I set down the Particulars in *Order of Time*; and if he shall chance to judge many of them to be trivial (as some perhaps will judge them all to be)as stand-ing by themselves, I desire him to consider, that, in Conjunction with the rest, they may be of some Moment; and that others may like to see those very Par-ticulars which he so little esteems. As to the *Year of our Lord*, (into which I change the *Years of the Kings Reigns*) I will not pretend to be most exact; as well be-cause I think it not much to the Purpose to be so, as also because each Year of a King's Reign does unavoidably fall into two Years of *our Lord*, and if I hit either of them, or come very near them, it answers my Intention.

In King *Ina*'s Laws, which were made betwixt 7 1 2,and 7 2 7, it is said, *Ovis cum Agno suo va-let unum Solidum, usque ad XIII Noctes post Pascha.* An Ewe, with her Lamb, is worth one Shilling, till 1 3 Nights after Ea-ster. *Bromton. Chr.* 766. but in-stead of 1 3, it should be 1 4, as it is in the *Saxon* of Mr. *Lambard.*

Between

Between the Years 900, and
1000, *Ednoth* bought 2 Hydes
of Land at *Stapleford* (in *Bed-
fordſhire*) for C. Shil. of the beſt
Silver, and gave them to *Ramſey
Abby*. D. *Gale*'s *Hiſt. Ramſ.*
415. and *p.* 471. *Hiſt. Elienſ.* a
Palfry was at X *s.* which was
about the Year 966. And *p.* 473.
an Acre of Land was purchaſed at
1 *s.* and a Hyde at C. *s.* from
whence one might think, that a
Hyde contained an 100 Acres,
but it contained 120 Acres. And,
once for all, you will do well to
remember, that a *Hyde*, a *Yard-
Land*, and a *Knight*'s *Fee*, contains no certain Number of Acres,
but differs according to different
Places; as you may ſee in the
Gloſſaries.

In the *Senatus Conſulta de Mon-
ticolis*, in the Time of King *Ethelred*, about the Year 1000, if a
Horſe be loſt, the Compenſation
muſt be 30 *s.* A Mare, or Colt
of a Year old, 20 *s.* A Mule
or young Aſſe at 12 *s.* An Ox
at 30 *d.* A Cow 24 *d.* A Swine
8 *d.* A Man one Pound. A
Sheep 1 *s.* A Goat at 11 *d.*
Note, That this is Saxon Money,

5 *d.*

5 *d.* to the Shill. and 48 *s.* to the Pound. *Whelock, p.* 96.

In 1043, *Chron. Saxon.* Corn was so dear, as no One ever remembred it; insomuch that a *Sester* of Wheat was sold for LX *d. H.* of *Huntingdon* explains this *Sextarius,* by saying it was as much as would load a Horse; and so does *Rob. de Monte,* in 1041. and both of them say it was sold for V *Sol.* And both of them lived about the Year 1140. A *Sester* or *Sextarius* was what we now call a *Quarter,* or a *Seam,* containing 8 Bushels. So Sir *H. Spelman.* And, in Confirmation of it, cites *Huntington,* L. 6. *Circa hoc tempus (scil. Ed. Confess.) tanta fames Angliam invasit, quod Sextarius Frumenti, qui Equo uni solet esse oneri, venundaretur V. Solidis, & etiam plus.* These two Authors, that wrote in *Latin,* and lived an 100 Years after, in the *Norman* Times, translated LX *d.* into V Sol. because in *their* Days the Shilling contained 12 *d.* But in the *Saxon* Times, *i. e.* when this Famine or Scarcity happened, 1043, the Shilling contained but 5 *d.* so that

LX *d.*

LX *d.* with the *Saxons* was XII
Sol. So the Fragment of *Æl-
fric Grammaticus* (cited by Mr.
Somner) who died, as Mr. *Whar-
ton* thinks, in *An.* 1051, *Anglia
Sacr.* P. I. *Libra on Leden is
Pund on Englifc, Fif Penegas ge-
macigath ænne Scillinge, & XXX
Penega ænne Mancs.* i. e. *Libra*
in Latin is a *Pound* in Englifh,
Five Pennies make *one* Schilling,
and 30 Pennies a *Mark.* A
Mark was therefore VI *Sol.* as I
have before obferved, becaufe
there are 6 times 5 in 30.

And it will not be amifs, to
hint to you, on this Occafion,
the Neceffity there is of remem-
bering how near your *Author* lived
to the Times he writes of ; becaufe moft Men are apt to fpeak
of Ages paft, according to the
Ways and Cuftoms of their own.
Thus, in the Laws of King *Athelftan,* as they are tranflated by
*John Brompton (inter X Scripto-
res) pag.* 847. an Offender is to
forfeit for his *firft* Fault, XXX *d.*
for his *fecond,* LX *d.* and for his
third, X *s.* Now this could not
poffibly be in King *Athelftan's*
Time, when LX *d.* made XII *s.*
but in *John Brompton's* Time,

(who

(who lived under *Ed.* III.) X *s.*
was double (as it ſtill is) to LX *d.*
and was a *treble* Mulct for a
third Offence, as reaſon required.
And thus in *L.* 59, of King *Ina,*
He who wounds or maims the
Horn of an Ox, is to pay X *d.*
[*Brompton* ſays V *d.*] of a Cow,
2 *d.* [*B.* ſays V *d.*] Who cuts off
the *Tail* of an Ox, is to pay IV *d.*
[*B.* ſays V *d.*] of a Cow, V *d.*
Who puts out the *Eye* of an Ox,
is to pay V *d.* of a Cow, a
Shilling. [*Brompton* ſays 12 *d.*]
Now, tho' a Shilling in *Bromp-*
ton's Time had in it 12 *d.* yet in
Ina's Time, it had but 5 *d.* I
could give you many Inſtances
of this Nature, if it were uſeful;
but theſe (which are not alien
from my Deſign) may ſuffice
to juſtify the Caution I gave you,
of minding your Author's Age.
But, leaving you to take part,
either with my Conjectures or
with the two above-named Authors, *Rob. de Monte,* and *H.*
Huntington, I ſet down the

	l.	*s.*	*d.*
Price of a Quarter of Wheat, in 1043, at ——— ——— —	oo	oo	60
In 1125, a *Sextar* or Quarter of Wheat, at ——— —	o1	oo	oo

So

So fay *Annales de Margan*
(put out by Dr. *Gale)* there was
fo great a Famine. But *H.
Huntington* in the fame Year
fays, *p.* 382. *Vendebatur Onus
equi frumentarium VIs.* And
Rob. de Monte, in the fame Year,
fays it was the deareft Year in
England, that was ever known;
for a Horfe-load of Wheat was
fold at VI *Sol.* This, upon the
Credit of thefe two Writers,
feems more likely than the
Price fet by the *Annalift,* of 20 *s.*

If the *Liber niger Schaccarii*
were written in the Time of *H.* I.
as fome affirm, it ought to be
noted down, in the next place,
(fince he began 1100, and ended 1135.)

	l.	*s.*	*d.*
1. *Pro Menfura Tritici ad Panem Centum Hominum.* ——	00	01	00
2. *Pro Corpore Bovis Pafcua-lis.* —— —— ——	00	01	00
Pro Præbenda XX Equorum.	00	00	04
3. *Pro Ariete vel Ove* ——	00	00	04

1. This was the Exchange
made by the King; that inftead
of *Provifions* for his Houfhold,
he might have fome ready *Money* to defray the Expences of his
Court, and pay his Soldiers. Inftead, therefore, of *Bread* for a

100 Men (for one Meal, I fuppofe) the Tenant was to pay a
Shilling.

2. Inftead of a ftalled Ox, the
Tenant was to pay a *Shilling*.
Mr. *Selden*, in his Notes on *Ead-
mer*, fays it was *five* Shillings.
But Sir *H. Spelman* (in v. *Firma)*
who faw the Book, and tranfcrib'd
this Paffage, puts it down *Solidum unum*; and him I follow.
He fays, it is a Book on which
the Sun does feldom fhine; meaning, that it is rarely feen and hard
to come at. He had the Opportunity of tranfcribing many
Pieces of it, which he has given,
in feveral Places of his *Gloffary*;
and fo has Mr. *Lownds* tranfcrib'd
a gcod deal of it, in his
Effay. But this is all that I could
find to my prefent Purpofe.

3. By *Provender* of Horfes is
always meant *Oats*. And inftead of bringing Oats for XX
Horfes (for a Night, I imagine)
the Tenant was to allow 4 Pence.

In the Laws of *H. I. cap.* 76.
Forty Sheep are valued at ———

l.	*s.*	*d.*
01	00	00

About the Year 1145, the Te-
nant of a Place was to pay yearly
XX *s*. or VII Oxen, each worth
III *s*. *M. Paris*, p. 1013.

In

In 1185, the Tenants of *Shireborn*, are, by Cuſtom, to pay either 2 *d.* or 4 *Hens*, which they will. And by the Cuſtom of *Beleſhall*, they are to have a *Ram*, or VIII *d.* (and in the Preface to King *Athelſtan*'s Laws, a *Ram* was at 4 *d. Vel unus Aries, qui valeat IIII Denarios.) Monaſt.* V. II. p. 528.

In 1196, ſo great a Scarcity of Corn that, at *Saliſbury*, a *Sema* of Wheat was ſold at———

In 1197, a *Sema* of Wheat *(i. e.* a Quarter) at ——— ———

	l.	*s.*	*d.*
	oo	13	04
	oo	18	08

Tho. Wikes, Chron. Dr. *Gale* (to whom we are obliged for the Edition of this, and other Hiſtorians) puts his Note under the Word *Sema, quatuor modios.* Which ſurely is not ſo; for *Sema* is a *Quarter*, or 8 Buſhel. And ſo Sir *H. Spelman, Seam VIII modiorum menſura*; ſic de Frumento dictum, quod unius Equi ſit Sauma, i. e. Sarcina. So that, with him, a *Quarter* of Wheat is a Horſe-load. And, doubtleſs, a *Quarter* is a quarter or *fourth* Part of ſome Load or Weight; for ſo *quarta, quartalis,* and *quartalium,* ſignifies a Peck, or the *fourth* Part of a Buſhel: and a

Quart

Quart is the *fourth* Part of a Gallon.

In 1199, King *John* ordered that a Tun of *Poictou* Wine fhould be fold for no more than——

A Tun of *Anjou* Wine at —

No *French* Wine above ——

Unlefs fo very good, that One would be glad to give, *per* Tun —— —— ——

No *Sextarium,* of *Poictou-* Wine, to be fold above ——

Nor any *White,* dearer than

	l.	*s.*	*d.*
	oi	oo	oo
	oi	o4	oo
	oi	o5	oo
	oi	o6	o8
	oo	oo	o4
	oo	oo	o6

But the Merchants could not bear this *Affize,* and fold the *Red* for 6 *d.* and the *White* for 8 *d.* the Gallon. *And the Land* (as the Hiftorian obferves) *was filled with Drink and Drunkards. Annales Burtonenfes. An.* 1199. Mr. *Stow* mentions no Meafure but a Gallon, for *Sextarius.* And Sir *H. Spelman* fays, that at *Paris,* a *Modius Vini* holds 36 *Sextarios,* and that a *Sextar* is 8 Pints. At this rate *Tonellus Vini* will hold but about 60 Gallons, which is the neareft to our *Hogf-head.* Mr. *Stow* calls the *Poictou* Wine, Wine of *Rochel:* And for the French Wine he fays the *Affize* was 1 *l.* 6 *s.* and 4 *d.* by the *Tun.* And fays, *p.* 165. that

they

they who fold by the *Tun*, *Hogf-head*, or otherwise, contrary to this Affize, were to be punifh-ed. But, if we are to underftand, in this place, a *Tun* of Englifh Meafure (which is 252 Gallons) by the Word *Tonellus*, then can-not a Gallon of *Poiɛtou* Wine come to 4 *d.* no, nor to 1 *d.* fince in XX*s.* there are but 240*d.* I fufpeɛt that *Sextarius* is more than a Gallon: for I do not think, that fo long ago as 1199, *Red* Wine at 1 *d. ob.* and *White* at 2 *d.* the Quart, would have filled the Land either with Drink or Drunkards; efpecially when *Anjou* and *Poiɛtou* were in the *Englifh*Hands; it muft be cheaper much, to make that Obferva-tion good. And tho' the *Rochel* Hogfhead be but 46 Gallons, yet it will not do.

In 1202, fo great a Scarcity (occafioned by continual Rains) that a *Quarter* of Wheat was fold for more than *(Annales, Waverl.)* ——— ——— ———

In 1205, there was fo great a Froft, lafting from *January* 14. to *March* 19. that Wheat was *(M. Paris)* the Quarter,——

l.	*s.*	*d.*
00	12	00
00	12	00

Mr.

Mr. *Stow* fays the Ground was fo hard, that it could not be tilled, and a Quarter of *Wheat* was fold the Summer following for a *Marc*; which, in *H.* II. Days, had ufually been at 1 *s.* *Beans* and *Peafe*, by the Quarter, 6 *s.* 8 *d.* And *Oats*, that were wont to be at 4 *d.* the Quarter, were now at 3 *s.* 4 *d.* *Fabian* puts Wheat, now, at 15 *s.*

In or about 1217, when the King came to *Redbourn*, the *Camerarius* of St. *Albans* loft three good Horfes, two Affes, and a good new Cart: all which were worth, at leaft, 50 *s.*

When *Fulco de Brent* came to *Langley*, the *Camerarius* loft three Houfes, that were burnt, and 35 Hogs, which all came to at leaft X *l.* and a Plow that coft X *s.* (which is a Miftake for X *d.*) And when the King of *France*'s *Marefchal* came, he loft many Oxen, Cows, Sheep, and other Things, and 24 Horfes, valued, at leaft, at 40 Marks, *i. e.* 26 *l.* 13 *s.* 4 *d.* *Matth. Paris*, page 1059. The *Camerarius* was the Receiver of the Rents, and who

provided

provided Clothes for the Monks.

In 1123, Wheat was very dear, and fold *per* Quarter, at *(Stow,* in 7 *H.* III.) —————

	l.	*s.*	*d.*
	00	12	00

About 1232, the *Abbot* of St. *Albans,* going a Journey, and attended with fix Efquires on Horfeback, agrees, that if the Horfes die on the Way, he will give for each Horfe X *s.* and the Horfes are to be ftrong and handfom; *decentes, & fortes ad portandum. M. Paris,* p. 1051.

In 1237, Wheat was by the

Quarter, —————	00	03	04
Barley, —————	00	02	00
Oats, ——— ———	00	01	00

Antiq. Peterborough, p. 304. Where I muft obferve, that I reduce all Meafures to a *Quarter,* for Uniformity's fake. Here I meet with the Word *Sceppe,* which the *Gloffaries* forget; but it fignifies a *Bufhel,* as appears, by cafting up the Sum here mentioned, where XXVIII *Quarter* and one *Sceppe* of Wheat are valued at 4 *l.* 13 *s.* 9 *d.* which is juft 5 *d.* the *Bufhel.*

If you chance to meet with any young Companions of yours, who flight thefe fort of Studies, you may acquaint them, that the

prefent

present excellent, moft learned,
and moft ufeful Bifhop of *Ely*,
put out, with no fmall Labour
of his own, the *Antiquities*, out
of which I have told you, what
Price, *Wheat* and *Barley*, and
Oats bare, in or about 1237. Or
(as Dr. *Kennet*) 1240.

	l.	s.	d.
In 1243, and 1244, Corn fo plentiful, that Wheat and Peafe were each of them by the Quarter *(M. Paris in Annis.)* ———	00	02	00
In 1246, a Quarter of Wheat (fo dear) at *(Tho. Wikes.)* ———	00	16	00
In 1247, a Quarter of Wheat (ftill dear) at *(Tho. Wikes.)* ———	00	13	04
In 1257, a Quarter of Wheat (exceffively dear) at *(Fabian)* —	01	04	00
In 1258, fo great a Famine, that many People were ftarved, fo that a Quarter of Wheat was fold at—— —— —— —	00	16	00

So *Walter Hemingford.* Which
makes me fufpect, that *Fabian*
was miftaken in his Accounts of
the foregoing Year, which make
Wheat *one third* dearer. Mr.
Stow fays, it was XV *s.* nay
XX *s.* the Quarter.

In 1270, Wheat was fo dear, that it was fold at, the Quarter,	4	16	00

And fometimes at 16 *s.* the
Bufh. which makes it at 6 *l.* 8 *s.*

So

So the *Author* of *Antiq. Bri-tan.* in *Vita Joh. Pecham.* who says that Provisions were so scarce, that Parents did eat their own Children. But, I hope, we need not believe him; 'tis only an Expression of the greatest Want imaginable.

	l.	*s.*	*d.*
In 1286, Wheat was at, the Quarter, —— —— ——	00	02	08

But such a Storm of Rain, Thunder, and Lightning, fell on St. *Margaret*'s Night, that Wheat came by degrees to the

Quarter, — — —— —	00	16	00

And this Dearness continued off and on for about 40 Years, so that sometimes it sold at *London* for 4 *l.* the Quarter. *H. Knyghton*, p. 2468.

In 1287, Wheat was so cheap, that it was sold at, the Quarter,	00	03	04

1288, So great the Plenty of Corn, and Scarcity of Money, that Wheat was sold, by the

Quarter, at — — — —	00	01	06

So *Angl. Sacr. Annales Wigorn.* The *Waverly Annals* say at 2 *s.* Mr. *Stow* says, that Wheat was sold (tho' the hottest Summer that was remembred) at *London* for 3 *s.* 4 *d.* in other Parts of *England*, at 1 *s.* 8 *d.* and 1 *s.* 4 *d.*

and

and 1 *s.* nay, in the *North* and *West* Parts, at 8 *d.* the Quarter. *Barley* at 6 *d.* and *Oats* at 4 *d.* and *Peafe* and *Beans* very cheap. And yet *Fabian* fets it down this Year at 9 *s.* 4 *d.* which is very dear. But it is eafy to be miftaken in fetting down one Year for another. And therefore when *H. Knyghton* fays, that great Dearnefs continued off and on, for 40 Years, we muft underftand him candidly; for now and then, it was, in that Space of Time, exceedingly cheap.

In 1289, *Walfingham* fays Wheat was fo cheap, that in fome Places it was fold, the Quarter at 1 *s.* 8 *d.* in others at 1 *s.* 4 *d.* and in others at 1 *s.* which does certainly belong to the Year foregoing. *Fabian* makes this a dear Year, and fays Wheat was by the Quarter at 12 *s.* and fays it went on increafing till it came in *Ed.* II. Time to 2 *l.* the Quarter.

It may be, Mr. *Dugdale*'s Account, in his *Warwickfhire Antiq.* may be the more likely, as being between the Extreams of *Walfingham* and *Fabian*, as follows:

Wheat,

	l.	*s.*	*d.*
Wheat, the Quarter, at———	oo	o6	oo
Rye — — — — —	oo	o5	oo
Barley — — — —	oo	o3	oo
Beans and Peafe — — —	oo	o2	o8
Oats — — — — —	oo	o2	oo
A Swan at — — — —	oo	o3	o4
A Duck at — — —	oo	oo	o1

Mr. *Stow*'s Account of this Year is, that by reafon of great Hail, and Rains, Wheat rofe from 2 *s.* the Quarter, to X *s.* 8 *d.* and, by degrees, came to XX *s.* the Quarter.

In 1290, *Tho. Walfingham,* and from him the Author of *Antiq. Britan.* in *Vita Joh. Pecham,* fays, that Wheat, which had been at 2 *s.* the Quarter, rofe (by reafon of great Rains and Storms) to — — — — | oo | 16 | oo |

Which Scarcity continued, off and on, for many Years.

In 1294, Wheat (dear) by the Quarter, *(Fabian)* — — | oo | 16 | oo |

And fometime XX *s.* as *H. Knyghton.*

In 1298, at *Scarborough* in *Yorkfhire,* the Price of an Ox | oo | o6 | o8 |

A Cow, at — — —	oo	o5	oo
A Heifer, at — — —	oo	o2	oo
A Sheep, at — — —	oo	oo	o1

Monafticon, Vol. 2. p. 403.

In

In 1299, This Year, was made an Act of *Common-Council*, for Prices of Victuals to be fold at *London*, by Confent of the King and Nobility: And as to Poultry, it was as follows. *Stow.*

	l.	*s.*	*d.*
A fat Cock — — —	oo	oo	01½
Two Pullets — — —	oo	oo	01½
A fat Capon — — —	oo	oo	02½
A Goofe — — — —	oo	oo	04
A Mallard — — —	oo	oo	01½
A Partrich — — —	oo	oo	01½
A Pheafant — — —	oo	oo	04
A Heron — — —	oo	oo	06
A Plover — — — —	oo	oo	01
A Swan — — — —	oo	03	oo
A Crane — — — —	oo	01	oo
Two Woodcocks — — —	oo	oo	01½
A fat Lamb, from *Chriftmafs* to *Shrovetide* — — —	oo	01	04
The fame, for all the Year after — — — —	oo	oo	04

In 1302, in *Dugdale*'s *Hift.* of *St.* Paul's, *page* 32. Wheat,

by the Quarter, at — —	oo	04	oo
Malt ground, at — — —	oo	03	04
Peafe, at — — — —	oo	02	06
Oats, at — — — —	oo	02	oo
A Bull, at — — —	oo	07	04
A Cow, at — — —	oo	06	oo
A fat Mutton, at — —	oo	01	oo
An Ewe Sheep, at —— —	oo	oo	08

A Capon,

	l.	*s.*	*d.*
A Capon, at ——— ———	oo	oo	o2
A Cock or Hen, —— ——	oo	oo	o1$\frac{1}{2}$

In 1309, *Will. Thorn (inter X. Scriptores)* in his *Chron. p.* 2010. gives us an Account of the Feaſt which *Ralf de Born, Prior* of St. *Auguſtine*'s, *Cant.* made on his Inſtallation-Day: In which it appears that he paid very great Rates for many Particulars of his Bill of Fare, conſidering the Times. I have given the Whole, but computed the Price of each Particular, that the Reader may ſee a little of the Spirit of that Age, and alſo what Proportion Commodities *then* bore, to what they do at this Day. And it will not be amiſs to give him the Preface which *William Thorn* makes to this Bill of Fare. *Be-cauſe* (ſays he) *the preſent Times* (1380) *may not, by any Means, be compared with the foregoing ones, for Plenty and Abundance of all ſorts of Things, I have thought it convenient to give the follow-ing Account of this Feaſt, not that Poſterity might imitate this Coſtlineſs, but rather might admire it.* And thus it was:

Of

	l.	*s.*	*d.*
Of Wheat, 53 Quarters, Price XIX *l.* [So that a Quarter came to ── ── ── ──	00	07	02
Of Malt, 58 Quart. Price XVII *l.* X *s.* [A Quarter at ──	00	06	00
Of Wine, 11 Tun, Price XXIIII *l.* [A Tun at or about	02	03	07½
Oats for the Guests, as well within as without the Gates of the City, 20 Quarters, Price IV *l.* [So that a Quarter came to ── ── ── ──	00	04	00
For Spice *(pro Speciebus)* XXVIII *l.*			
For CCC *l.* of Wax, Price VIII *l.* [So that a Pound came to near ── ── ──	00	00	06½
Almonds, D *l.* Price III *l.* XVIII *s.* [So that a Pound came to above ── ── ──	00	00	01¼
XXX Ox Carcasses *(pro Carcoisis Boum)* Pr. XXVII *l.* [Each came to ── ── ──	00	18	00
Of Hogs, C. Price XVI *l.* [So that each Hog came to about	00	03	02¼
Of Muttons, [*de Multonibus*] CC. Price XXX *l.* [Each came to ── ── ──	00	03	00
Of Geese, [*de Aucis*] M. Price XVI *l.* [Each Goose about ──	00	00	03¼
Of Capons and Hens, D. Price VI *l.* V *s.* [Each Fowl came to ── ── ──	00	00	03

Of

	l.	s.	d.

Of Pullets, [*de Pulonibus*] CCCCLXXIII. Price III *l.* XIV *s.* [Each — — —   00   00   01½

Of Pigs, [*de Porcellis*] CC. Price V *l.* [Each Pig at — —   00   00   06

Of Swans, 24. Price VII *l.* [Each Swan came to — —   00   05   10

Of Rabbits, 600. Pr. XV *l.* [Each Rabbit came to — —   00   00   06

De Scentis de Braun, 16. Price III *l.* V *s.* Each *Shield of Brawn* (and therefore Mr. *Somner* gueffes right, that it fhould be read *Scutis*) came to — — —   00   04   00 ¼

Of Partrich, Mallards, Bitterns *(Butores)* and Larks, XVIII *l.*

Of Earthen Pots, M. Price XV *s.*

Of Salt, 9 Quart. Price X *s.* 'tis 9 *Summas.* But 'tis, without doubt, a Miftake; for Salt was never fo low as *Three-Half-Pence* the *Bufhel.*

De Sciphis, M. CCCC *Mugs*, I believe, or *Wooden Cans* to drink in, or it may be *Black Jacks.*

Difhes and Platters, [*Platellis*] or Trenchers, M.M.M.CCC.

De Scopis & Gachis. Price VIII *l.* IV *s. Scopa* is a Broom or Beefom, and, by its Ufe, a Penitentiary *Difcipline.* But what

it

it is here, or what *Gachis* signifies, I know not.

Of Fiſh, Cheeſe, Milk, O-
nions, &c. Price II*l.* X*s.*

Eggs, 9600, Pr. IV*l.* X*s.*
Which are about 9 for ── ──

Of Saffron [*Crocus*] and Pep-
per. Price I*l.* XIV*s.*

In Coals, and [*Doleis*] ſetting
up Furnaces. Price II*l.* VIII*s.*

In CCC Ells of Caneum, Can-
vas, or Flax. Pr. IV*l.*

In making up Tables, Treſ-
ſels, and Dreſſers. Price I*l.* XIV*s.*

Given to the Cooks and their
Boys, VI*l.*

To the Minſtrels, or Mu-
ſick, III*l.* X*s.*

The Sum total is,
CCLXXXVII*l.* VII*s.* taking
in the Preſents and Gratuities. At
this Feaſt there were 6000 Gueſts
that ſat down at the Tables, and
they had 3000 Meſſes. And
therefore inſtead of *quo reſpon-
dentes* (at the End of this Account) I would read *Correſpon-
dentes :* anſwering to, or ſetting
Oppoſite to each other. And ſo
there was a Meſs to each Couple.
I obſerv'd above, that this *Prior*
paid dear for many Particulars;
and if you will compare this

l.	*s.*	*d.*
oo	oo	oi

Account

Account with the foregoing ones, you will find his *Corn* of each kind, his *Beef*, and *Mutton*, and *Swans*, to be at a high Rate: and as for the Article of *Rabbits*, I am almoſt ſure there muſt be ſome Miſtake in it, for they could never be ſo dear (ſo long ago) as 6 *d.* a piece.

	l.	*s.*	*d.*
In 1309, a pair of Shoes, (*Spel. Gl. v. Vatarius*) at —	oo	oo	o4

In 1314, *Antiq. Oxon.* Upon the Chancellors and Proctors Complaints to the King, (*E.* II.) that the Market of *Oxford* ran unreaſonably high, ſo that poor Scholars could hardly live, the King ſent down his *Mandate*, to regulate this Affair. But ſince the *Parliament* took the ſame Thing (with reſpect to the whole Nation) into Conſideration, it will be better to give the Rates they thought fit to ſet upon Proviſions, eſpecially ſince there is no Difference, or but a little, betwixt theſe two Accounts. Thus therefore Mr. *Stow* ſets it down.

	l.	*s.*	*d.*
A ſtalled or Corn-fed Ox, at	o1	o4	oo
A Graſs-fed Ox, — —	oo	16	oo
A fat ſtall'd Cow, — —	oo	12	oo
An ordinary Cow, — —	oo	1o	oo

A fat

	l.	*s.*	*d.*
A fat Mutton, unſhorn (Corn-fed, the *Oxford Antiq.* ſay) —	00	01	08
A fat Mutton, ſhorn —	00	01	02
A fat Hog of two Years old (the *Antiq.* ſay it ſhould be *ovis bima*. But, I think, the Price does not ſo well agree with that) at — — — — —	00	03	04
A fat Gooſe in the City, 3 *d.* but every where elſe, at —	00	00	02½
A fat Capon, in the City, 2 *d.* ½, elſewhere, at — —	00	00	02
A fat Hen, in the City, 1 *d.* ½, elſewhere, at — — --	00	00	01
2 Chickens, in the City 1 *d.* ½, elſewhere, at — ——	00	00	01
4 Pigeons (in the City but 3 Pigeons) for — — —	00	00	01
24 Egs (in the City but 20) for	00	00	01

But notwithſtanding this *Act of Parliament*, Things could not be purchaſed at theſe Rates, for People would not bring them to Market, (and that is a thing Parliaments cannot remedy) and ſo the King was fain to revoke the former *Act*, and leave People to ſell as they could (for a Trade will do as it can, and never be forced, one way or other) and (as *Walſingham* tells us, in 1315, and 1316,) the Price of Peaſe

and

	l.	*s.*	*d.*
and Beans, and of Wheat, was, by the Quarter, at ⸺ ⸺	01	00	00
Malt, at ⸺ ⸺ ⸺	00	13	04
Salt, at ⸺ ⸺ ⸺	01	15	00

Nay (by the Rains in Harveſt) the Dearth was ſuch, that Wheat came to 30, and 40 *s.* the Quarter. And Good Ale was at the Gallon *(per Lagenam,* from whence the Word *Flaggon,* which uſed heretofore to hold 4 Quarts, is derived) ⸺ ⸺ ⸺ ⸺ 00 00 02

The better ſort, at ⸺	00	00	03
And the beſt of all, at ⸺	00	00	04

So that a Proclamation was fain to be iſſued out, that a *Lagena* of Ale ſhould be ſold at— 00 00 01

And that no Wheat ſhould be malted *(imbraſiatum)* which the *Londoners* had uſually done, to the great Conſumption of Corn, and ſold it at (the Flaggon) 00 00 01½

And the viler Ale, at ⸺ 00 00 01

In 1316, Wheat exceeding dear *(Fabian)* at the Quarter,— 01 12 00

In 1317, ſo great a Scarcity of Corn, that at *Leiceſter,* on a *Saturday,* Wheat was ſold at *(per* Quarter) ⸺ ⸺ ⸺ 02 04 00

And the *Friday* following, at the ſame Place, at 14 *s.* the Quarter.

So

So *H. Knyghton*; but there is a Miftake in his faying, the Scarcity continued for two Years, and was general throughout all *England.* *Fabian* puts it this Year, ——— — — —   02 13 04

And yet of this very Year 1317, *Stow* tells us, that the Harveft was in fo early, that all was houfed before St. *Giles*'s Day, which is *Septemb.* 1, and Wheat, that was before at IV *l.* the Quarter, was now at VI *s.* VIII *d.* and Oats, that was before III *l.* IV *d.* now at V *s.* IV *d.* which makes what *Knyghton* fays probable; for what he fays, was but a Decreafe of *two thirds:* Whereas Mr. *Stow*'s Decreafe is *eleven in twelve.*

In 1326, 1 *Ed.* III. at *Tunbridge* in *Kent, Inquifitio unum Capitale Meffuagium* LXX Acres of Arable Land, worth *per An.* XXXV *s.*

	l.	*s.*	*d.*
Twelve Hens, at ———	00	01	06
One Cock and 13 Hens, at—	00	01	07
Eight Porkers and a half, at	00	15	00
80 Acres of Arable, at XX *s.*			
i. e. per Acre ——— ———	00	00	03
20 Acres of Pafture, each Acre at ——— — ———	00	00	01
14 Acres of Meadow, each at	00	00	04

18 Acres

	l.	s.	d.
18 Acres of Arable, each Acre at —— —— ——	oo	oo	o3
27 Acres of Arable, each at	oo	oo	o4
Two Acres of Meadow, each Acre at —— —— ——	oo	oo	10
A Cock — — — ---	oo	oo	o1
Three Hens — — —	oo	oo	o4$\frac{1}{2}$

Mr. *Lambard*'s *Perambulation of* Kent, *p.* 541. You may fee from hence, that you can make no certain Computation, from the Rates of Acres, becaufe of the Difference of the Grounds.

In 1336, fuch Plenty of Corn, and Scarcity of Money, that Wheat was, at *London*, by the Quarter ——

	l.	s.	d.
Quarter — — ——	oo	o2	oo
A fat Ox, at — ——	oo	o6	o8

So *H. Knyghton.* And *Fabian* adds,

	l.	s.	d.
For a fat Sheep VI *d.* and at moft —— —— — —	oo	oo	o8
VI Pigeons for —— ---	oo	oo	o1
A fat Goofe, at —— ——	oo	oo	o2
A Pig —— —— ——	oo	oo	o1

And fays it was occafioned by King *E.* III. gathering up all the Money he could get, to carry on his Wars in *France* and *Scotland*.

In 1338, Wheat, the Quarter, at

	l.	s.	d.
ter, at —— —— —	oo	o3	o4
Barley, at —— ——	oo	oo	10

Peafe

	l.	*s.*	*d.*
Peaſe and Beans, the Quarter, at ——— ——— ———	00	01	00
Oats, the Quarter, at ———	00	00	10

In 1339, ſeveral Undertakers promiſe to deliver at the Town of *Berwick*, and in *Leith-Road*, 10000 Quarters of Wheat and

Malt, each Quarter at ——	00	09	00
Oats, Beans, and Peaſe, each Quarter at ——— ———	00	05	00

Sir *R. Cotton*'s *Abridgm. Records.* This was a high Price.

In 1343, Two Oxen, Price

of each ——— ———	00	08	00
In 1344, One Cow, at———	00	05	00

Dr. *Kennet*'s *Paroch. Antiq.*

In 1348, *H. Knyghton* ſays, that in the Peſtilence, Things were ſold almoſt for nothing. A

Horſe worth 40 *s.* was ſold for	00	06	08
A good fat Ox, at ——— ——	00	04	00
A Cow, at ——— ——	00	01	00
An Heifer, or Steer, at———	00	00	06
A fat Mutton, at ———	00	00	04
An Ewe, at ——— ———	00	00	03
A Lamb, at ——— ———	00	00	02
A Hog, at ——— ———	00	00	05
A Stone of Wooll, at ———	00	00	09

The Hiſtorian ſays upon this Matter, *Erat leve precium cunctis, præ mortis timore,* p. 2599, they were not only afraid of the Cattles dying, but of their own, for,

otherwiſe,

otherwise, *Wooll* need not have
been so cheap.

In 1349, Corn so plentiful,
and other Provisions, that Wheat
was, by the Quarter, at ———

A fat Ox at *London*, for ———
Antiquit. Britann.

In 1359, Wheat, very dear,
a Quarter, at *(Fabian)* ———

In 1361, Wheat so cheap,
that a Quarter was at (*Monast.*
V. 2.) ——— ——— ———

Two Hens for ——— ———

In 1363, a Widow is to pay
4 Hens, or in Money ———

XII Hogs at XVIII s. each
Hog at ——— ——— ---
Dr. *Kennet's Paroch. Antiq.*

Yet Wheat so dear, that *Walfingham* says a Quarter was at

In 1369, *Walfingham* says
there was such a Dearth, that
Wheat was sold, by the Quarter,
at 1 *l.* 4 *s.* according to *Stow* —

Barley, at ——— —

Oats, at ——— ———

In 1379, Wheat so cheap,
that the Quarter was at ———

White Wine was sold by the
Gallon, for ——— —

Red Wine by the Gallon, at
(Stow) ——— ———

	l.	*s.*	*d.*
	oo	o2	oo
	oo	o6	o8
	o1	o6	o8
	oo	o2	oo
	oo	oo	o1
	oo	oo	o4
	oo	o1	o6
	oo	15	oo
	o1	oo	oo
	oo	16	o4
	oo	o8	oo
	oo	o4	oo
	oo	oo	o6
	oo	oo	o4

In

	_l._	_s._	_d._
In 1382, a Tun of Wine not to exceed *(Stow)*——— —	04	00	00
In 1387, Barley, at *Leicefter*, fold by the Quarter, at ———	00	01	00
Wheat, by the Quarter, at	00	02	00
Barley, in the fame Year, by the Quarter, at—— ——	00	02	00
Peafe, by the Quarter, at —	00	01	00
Siliginis, (which, what it is, I know not) *per* Quarter, at	00	01	00
In 1390, Wheat at *Leicefter*, by the Quarter, at ———	00	16	08

and 14 _s._ and 13 _s._ 4 _d._ And Wooll was fo cheap (by reafon of a Law that forbad Men to carry it but to fuch and fuch Places, for Stranger-Merchants to fetch it, and might not export it themfelves) that it was fold, by the Stone, at ———

	00	03	00

and at 2 _s._ and 1 _s._ 8 _d._ (*H. Knyghton,* who lived at *Leicefter*.)

In 1401, Wheat very dear, the Quarter at *(Fabian)* ———

	00	16	00

In 1407, in a *Computus,* relating to the *Prior* and *Canons* of *Burcefter Oxf.* are found thefe following Particulars, to our prefent Purpofe, which I have tranfcribed out of Dr. *Kennet*'s *Parochial Antiquities*; which Book, if you will read it, will pay you for your Time and Pains,

being

being full of many curious, learned, and useful Obfervations, in
this way of Learning.

	l.	*s.*	*d.*
For a Cow,	oo	07	oo
For the Calf of that Cow,—	oo	o1	o8
For a Calf of a Cow that was fomewhat weak, *debilis*,	oo	o1	oo
For 5 Calves (each at 2s. 1d. ½, very near)	oo	10	o8
For 5 Bufhels and a half of Salt,	oo	o3	o4½
For a Cowele or Cooler, in Brewing,	oo	oo	o9
For a Cow and her Calf,—	oo	07	o6
For 2 Bufhels of Wheat,	oo	oo	10
For a Man threfhing for V Days	oo	oo	10
For 2 Oxen	o1	o6	o8
For one Ox	oo	11	o6
For a new Plow,	oo	oo	10
For XI Bufhel of Sowing-Wheat (the Quarter near 4s. 4d. ¾.)	oo	o5	10¼
For XVIII Bufh. of Sowing-Oats, (the Quart. at 2 s.)	oo	o4	o6
For a Dung-Cart, and all that belong'd to it,	oo	o1	o2
For a Pair of Cart-wheels,—	oo	o3	o2
For R. P. working XII Days (3 d. per Day)	oo	o3	oo
For J. B. working one Day	oo	oo	o3
For a Calf	oo	o1	o7
In 1416, Wheat very dear, the Quarter at *(Fabian)*	oo	16	oo

In

	l.	s.	d.
In 1423, Wheat cheap, the Quarter at *(Fabian)* —— ——	oo	o8	oo
Malt, at —— —	oo	o5	oo

Wheat at 8 *s.* the Quarter, was not, for thofe Times, *cheap;* but it was cheap, with refpect to fome dear Years foregoing.

A Ram, at —— —	oo	oo	o8
A Cheefe, at ——	oo	oo	o4

From fuch Articles as this laft foregoing one, where neither *Weight* nor *Goodnefs* is expreffed, nothing can be concluded.

In 1425, in another *Computus* of the *Prior* and a *Canon* of *Burcefter Oxf.* in Dr. *Kennet*'s *Par. Ant.*

For a Colt fold, —— —	oo	o8	oo
For X Quarter of Peafe, (each Quarter at 2 *s.* 2 *d.*) at — —	oɪ	oɪ	o8
For XVIII Quarters and 2 Bufh. of Peafe (about 3 *d.* ⅛ *per* Bufh.) at —— ——	oɪ	17	o7
For V Ox-Hides ——	oo	12	oo
For II Cow-Hides ——	oo	o2	o7
For III Cow-Hides ——	oo	o4	o8
For XVI Calves-Skins ——	oo	o2	oo
For XXI Lambs—— ——	oo	o4	oo
For XXXVI Sheep-Skins, of 2 Years old —— ——	oo	o9	oo
For XXIII Tod of pureWooll (at 9 *s.* 6 *d.* the Tod) ——	ɪo	18	o6

For

	l.	*s.*	*d.*
For XIX Ells of Cloth for Napkins ——— ———	00	05	00
For CXXXII Flaggons and an half of Ale, at ———	00	04	10

I have obſerv'd before, that *Lagena,* (a Flaggon) holds 4 Quarts. Now an 132 Flaggons muſt, at that Rate make 528 Quarts, for which there was paid but 58 Pence: which will bring it to 9 Quarts a Penny, and 6 will remain beſides. Now this cannot be allowed; there is therefore a Miſtake either in ſetting down the Number of the Flaggons, or of the Money paid for them. And ſuch Miſtakes are very eaſy. A Flaggon of Ale, or a Gallon, was (at or near this time) valued at 1 *d.* or 1 *d.* $\frac{1}{4}$, or 1 *d.* $\frac{1}{2}$. And if you compute at this laſt Rate, and reckon XV *s.* for IV, it will come pretty near the Matter.

For XXXII Flaggons of Red Wine, at 8 *d.* the Flaggon, —	01	01	04
For III Flaggons and III Quarts of Sweet Wine, at 1 *s.* 4 *d.* the Flaggon ——— ———	00	05	00

This is a manifeſt Proof, that *Lagena* holds 4 Quarts; for if it had held 3, there had been 4

Lagenæ

Lagenæ ; if it held 2, there had been 4 *Lagenæ* and 1 Quart. A Quart came to 4 *d.*

	l.	*s.*	*d.*
To *W. H.* a Stone-cutter, for 4 Days work (4 *d.* the Day) —	oo	o1	o4
To *J. C.* and 2 Servants, Tyling for 4 Days (between 3 *d.* and 4 *d.*)	oo	o3	o4
To two Sawyers working X Days (4 *d.* the Day)	oo	o6	o8
For XX Pullets —	oo	o1	o8
For a Quarter of an Ox to falt	oo	o1	o4
For a Cade of Red Herrings (720 the Cade)	oo	o8	oo
For a Frail of Figs —	oo	o3	o4
For 12 Pound of Raifins —	oo	o1	o1
For a great Flefh-Ax —	oo	o1	o4
For 2 Yards of Ruffet Cloth for the Shepherd	oo	o2	o2
For 4 Quarters of Wheat to be malted, ('tis *pro 4 quarteriis Frumenti pro Brafio faciendo*)	oo	16	oo
each Quarter at —	oo	o4	oo
For a Bay-Horfe, for the Prior's Stable —	o1	o6	o8
For 2 Colts —	oo	o9	oo
For 30 Pair of Autumnal (Winter) Gloves for the Servants —	oo	o4	oo
To the Baker's Servant for X Days —	oo	o1	oo
For threfhing a Quarter of Wheat —	oo	oo	o3½

For

	l.	*s.*	*d.*
For 8 Woodcocks, for a Prefent	00	01	00
For XII Pair of Gloves to the Bp. of *Worcefter*'s Servants——	00	05	00
For one Man plowing and harrowing 12 Days —— —	00	01	00
Vaccæ Pretium, (*Maddox Formul.* p. 144.) at —— —	00	08	00
In 1426, V Oxen, each apprais'd at —— —— —	00	03	04
VI Cows, each at ——	00	02	08
III Horfes, each at ———	00	03	00

Sir *H. Spelman, Gloffary V. Graile.*

In 1434, the Autumn was fo wet, that for almoft two Years following, in many Places of the Kingdom, Wheat was fold, the Quarter, at —— ——   01 06 08

And yet at the End of the Year following it came again to (*Hift. Croyland Continuatio*) 5 *s.* 4 *d.* therefore feems to have been the ufual common Price of a Quarter, about that time.   00 05 04

In 1439, *Stow* fays, there was fuch Scarcity, that Wheat was fold at 1 *l.* the Quarter. *Fabian,* at—— —— ——   01 06 08

In 1440, The Scarcity continued, Wheat was, the Quarter, at —— —— ——   01 04 00

Malt, the Quarter, at ——   00 13 00

Oats

	l.	*s.*	*d.*
Oats, the Quarter ——	00	05	04
Wine, by the Gallon ——	00	01	00
Bay Salt, by the Bushel——	00	01	00

If I am not misinformed, the Statutes of a *College*, that was founded much about the same Time with yours, say, that the weekly Allowance, for every *Fellow*, *Chaplain*, and *Scholar*, shall be 1 *s.* 4 *d.* and in Times of Scarcity, 1 *s.* 5 *d.* and 1 *s.* 6 *d.* But if Corn should be (and continue for 20 Days) above 2 *s.* the Bushel, then their Allowance shall be 1 *s.* 8 *d.* the Week, and no farther. Wheat therefore at XVI *s.* the Quarter, must be accounted exceedingly dear. And yet in *An.* 1440, it was, at the lowest reckoning of Mr. *Stow*, at 20 *s.* the Quarter. But, indeed, from that Year, to 1460, I have never found Wheat at above 8 *s.* the Quarter, and therefore 2 *s.* the Bushel might well be accounted a very high Price. And here, if it would avail me any thing, I might justly bemoan our want of History for these last 250 Years, and upwards, (I mean of Latin Writers) there having been very few, that

have

have tranfmitted any thing (as of
their own knowledge) of the
Reigns of *H.* IV, V, VI, *Ed.*
IV, V, *Rich.* III. except what
Sir *Thomas More* has left us of
the two laft. But, as to the
Purpofe in Hand, I have had
the good Fortune to meet with
the *Computus*'s of 9 or 10 Years,
that will exactly fit you, in this
Inquiry, and they are of very
great Credit, and fhall go under
the Name of *E. C.* but I will
firft give you an Account of
the Price of Things, which I
received from a private, but a
very creditable hand, of the Year
1444.

	l.	*s.*	*d.*
For an 100 Quarters of Wheat 21 *l.* 13 *s.* 4 *d.* each Quarter at	00	04	04
For 2 Bufhels of Wheat, (I fuppofe for Seed) —— ——	00	01	00
For 2 Bufhels of Peafe (for Seed alfo) —— —— —	00	01	00
For 5 Quarters of Peafe, 15 *s.* each Quarter at —— — —	00	03	00
For 50 Quarter of Malt, 10 *l.* each Quarter at —— ——	00	04	00
For 6 Calves, 12 *s.* each Calf at —— —— —— —	00	02	00

For

	l.	*s.*	*d.*
For 8 Porkers, 1 *l.* 4 *s.* each at —— —— —— — befides (*i. e.* without) the Head.	oo	o3	oo
For 40 Geefe, 10 *s.* each Goofe at —— —— ——	oo	oo	o3
For 31 Dozen of Pigeons, 10 *s.* 8 *d* each Dozen at about	oo	oo	o4 $\frac{3}{4}$
For 15 Doz. of Pigeons, 7 *s.* 6 *d.* each Doz. at—— ——	oo	oo	o6
For 100 Dozen of Pidgeons, each Doz. at —— —— —	oo	oo	o5 $\frac{1}{2}$
For an Ox —— ——	o1	11	o8
For 8 Cignets, or young Swans, each —— ——	oo	o3	oo
For a Flitch of Bacon ——	oo	o1	o8
For 4 Oxen (young I fup-pofe, and lean) 52 *s.* each at——	oo	13	oo
For 26 Warp of Ling——	o1	1o	o4
For 100 Stock-Fifh ——	oo	17	o6
For a Barrel of Herrings, (*i. e.* 30 Gallons fully packed)——	o1	oo	oo
For 2 Plough-Oxen ——	o1	o3	oo
For a Quarter of Oats——	oo	o1	o8
For three Bufhel of Green Peafe (for Seed) —— ——	oo	o2	o3

At this Time it appears that Mafter Traders wrought by the Day at 3 *d.* and their Labourers or Servants at 1 *d.* But then, I be-lieve, they had their Meat and Drink. The yearly Wages were, fome 1 *l.* 6 *s.* 8 *d.* others 1 *l.* For this, fee hereafter, *Chap.* 5.

In

In 1445, VII Quarter and an half of Wheat came to XXX s. which is, each Quarter, at ——

	l.	s.	d.
which is, each Quarter, at ——	00	04	06
Oats, by the Quarter, at ——	00	02	00
XII Flaggons, or Gallons of Ale I s. VI d. each Gallon at ——	00	00	01 $\frac{1}{2}$
Hay, by the Load———	00	03	06 $\frac{1}{2}$
For 3000 Red Herrings ——	01	11	00
XXIV Bullocks and Heifers, VI l. each Head at——— ——	00	05	00
Cloth for Surplices for Scholars, the Ell, at——— —— ——	00	00	08

And, that you may not think this Cloth to be very coarse, I assure you it was the same with the *Napkins* used at the *Altar*; and that, if you know the Religion of those Days, was certainly fine. *E. C.*

	l.	s.	d.
In 1447, Wheat, by the Quarter, *E. C.* —— —	00	08	00
Oats, the Quarter ——	00	02	01 $\frac{1}{2}$
In 1448, Wheat, by the Quarter —— ——	00	06	08
Oats, the Quarter ——	00	02	00
A Cade of Red Herrings —	00	05	08
A Barrel of White Herrings, *E. C.* —— —— ——	00	09	03
In 1449, Wheat, by the Quarter, *E. C.* — — ——	00	05	00
Cade of Red Herrings ——	00	06	00
Barrel of White Herrings —	00	10	03

XV

	l.	s.	d.
XV Sheep, at I l. XVI s. X d. each Sheep at (within ½.) ——	oo	o2	o5½
VII Hogs, at XIII s. VIII d. each Hog at (within ½.)——	oo	o1	11½
In 1450, Oats, the Quarter	oo	o1	10
Beans, the Quarter ——	oo	o2	o6
In 1451, Wheat, by the Quarter, at —— —— --	oo	o8	oo
Oats, the Quarter ——	oo	10	10¼
XXVI Gallons of Ale, (here the Word *Galo* is ufed for *Lagena*) 3 s. each Gallon at ——	oo	oo.	o1½
Beans, the Quarter —— —	oo	o3	o4
For a Cade of Red Herrings	oo	o7	o4
For a Barrel of White Herrings, *E. C.* —— —— —	oo	13	o7
In 1453, Wheat, by the Quarter —— —— ——	oo	o5	o4
Ale, *per* Gallon —— —	oo	oo	o1¼
Cade of Red Herrings ——	oo	o7	o6
Fourfcore White Herrings, *E. C.*—— —— —— —	oo	o1	oo
In 1454, Oats, by the Quarter—— —— —— ——	oo	o1	10½
In 1455, Wheat very cheap, the Quarter at —— ——	oo	o1	o2
Malt, the Quarter (Mr. *Stow)* at —— —— —— —	oo	o1	o5
In 1457, Wheat by the Quart.	oo	o7	o8
Oats, the Quarter —— —	oo	o1	o9¾
A Gallon of Ale —— —	oo	oo	o1
A Cade of Red Herrings, at	oo	o6	o8
92 White Herrings, *E. C.*——	oo	o1	oo

In

In 51 *H*. III. it was determined by *Authority*, that when
a Quarter of Barley was fold at
2 *s*. then *Ale* might be afforded
4 Quarts for 1 *d*. And when
Barley was at 2 *s*. 6 *d*. the Quarter, then Ale was to be 7 Quarts
for 2 *d*. and fo to increafe and
decreafe, after the Rate of 6 *d*.
the Quarter. But no Rules
can always hold for Trade:
as you may fee, by comparing the
Price of Barley and Ale, in thefe
and other Accompts.

	l.	*s.*	*d.*
In 1459, Wheat, by the Quarter ——— ——— ———	00	05	00
Oats, the Quarter ——— —	00	08	10
A Gallon of Ale, at ———	00	00	01
A Cade of Red Herrings, at	00	07	10½
92 White Herrings, at *E. C.*	00	01	00
In 1460, Wheat the Quarter, at ——— ——— —	00	08	00
Oats, the Quarter ———	00	02	00
A Gallon of Ale, at ———	00	00	01
Cade of Herrings, at———	00	07	00
192 White Herrings, at, *E. C.* ——— ——— —	00	02	00

Here my private Guide, for
a while, leaves me; but not before it has made my Obfervation
good, that from 1440, to 1460
(the Time you inquire after)
Wheat was never above 8 *s*. the

Quarter,

Quarter, notwithstanding the Sword was drawn betwixt the Houses of *York*, and *Lancaster*, which usually cuts down Corn, as well as Men.

In 1463, It was enacted in Parliament, that no Corn should be imported, if Wheat were not above 6 s. 8 d. Rye 4 s. Barley 3 s. the Quarter; which signifies those Prices to be high.

	l.	s.	d.
In 1463, At *London*, Wheat was, by the Quarter ———	00	02	00
Barley, the Quarter ———	00	01	10
Pease, the Quarter ———	00	03	04
Oats, the Quarter ————	00	01	02
At *Norfolk* the same Year, Wheat, the Quarter — —	00	01	08
Barley — — —	00	01	00
Malt ——— ———	00	01	08
Oats, Mr. *Stow* ———	00	01	00
In 1464, White Wheat was sold by the Quarter (Sir *R. Cotton*'s Records) ——— ———	00	06	08
In 1475, Oats, the Quarter, at ——— ——— ———	00	01	10
Load of Hay, at ———	00	06	08

This is from a *private Computus*, *P. C.*

In 1486, Wheat, very dear; and Bay-Salt the same Price.

Fabian.——— ——— ———	01	04	00

In

	l.	*s.*	*d.*
In 1489, Oats, the Quarter, *P. C.*	oo	o2	oo
In 1491, Wheat, the Quarter, *Fabian*	oo	14	o8
In 1493, Oats, the Quarter	oo	o2	oo
Beans, *P. C.*	oo	o3	o4
In 1494, Wheat (cheap and Bay-Salt the fame) *Fabian*	oo	o4	oo
In 1495, Wheat, *Fabian*	oo	o3	o4
White Herrings, the Barrel, *Fabian*	oo	o3	o4
In 1497, Wheat (very dear) *Fabian*	o1	oo	oo
Oats, the Quarter, *P. C.*	oo	o2	oo
In 1498, Load of Hay, *P. C.*	oo	o8	o2

Mr. *Stow* fays Hay was ufually at 5 *s.* but now it was 10 *s.* or 12 *s.*

In 1499, Wheat, *per* Quart.	oo	o4	oo
Bay-Salt, the Quarter	oo	o2	o8
A Tun of Gafcoign Wine, at, Mr. *Stow*	o2	oo	oo

It is not for want of Pains, that you have no fuller Accounts of thefe foregoing 40 Years; for, I think, few publick Books have efcaped my Diligence; and my private Ones have proved as barren. And fo it will be for the 40 Years and more that follow; our *Chroniclers* wanted the Care and Obfervation of their Predeceffors; and fetting up for

Politicians,

Politicians, quite neglected (as
they thought them) leſſer Matters. And, by a ſtrange Fortune I have read the *Computus's*,
or Accompts, of a *Publick Body*,
where there was always good
Houſe-keeping, and have not
yet been able, for the Space of 40
Years, to find what Price a Quarter of Wheat bore, tho' they
ſpent a great many every Month.
Your College-Books may ſupply
theſe Wants, if you will now
and then relax from Studies
of more Attention, to inſpect
theſe lighter Matters, which will
not make you a leſs uſeful Mem-
ber of your Society.

In 1504. *Antiq. Canterb. Ap-
pendix*, p. 27. Wheat, the Quarter, at

	l.	*s.*	*d.*
Wheat, the Quarter, at	00	05	08
Red Wine, *per Dolium*	04	00	00
Claret Wine, *per Dolium*	03	13	04
White Wine, elect	03	06	08
Malveſy, a Butt	04	00	00
Ale of *London*, per *Dol.*	01	10	00
Ale of *Canterbury* per *Dol.*	01	05	00
Beer, *per Dol.*	01	03	04

Dolium, I believe, does here
ſignify a *Pipe*, or *Butt*, which
contains an 126 Gallons. So
that the Ale of *London* comes to

very

	l.	*s.*	*d.*
very near 3 *d.* the Gallon. The Red Wine at 7 *d.* ½.			
In 1505, A Load of Hay, at	00	06	00
Oats, by the Quarter, at—	00	03	00
In 1506, Oats, by the Quarter, at	00	02	00
Beans, the Quarter, at	00	03	08
In 1507, Oats, the Quarter	00	02	00
Beans, the Quarter — —	00	03	06
A Hogfhead of Red Wine	01	06	08
In 1508, Oats, the Quarter	00	01	10
In 1510, Oats —	00	02	00
Load of Hay — —	00	09	00
In 1511, Load of Hay —	00	05	00
Beans, the Quarter, at—	00	03	04
Oats — — —	00	02	00
In 1512, Oats, the Quarter	00	02	00
Beans — — — —	00	04	00
In 1513, Oats — — —	00	02	04
In 1515, Beans, *P. C.* —	00	04	02
In 1521, A Dearth. Wheat was by the Quarter (Mr *Stow)*	01	00	00
In 1526, Oats, the Quarter	00	03	00
Beans, at — — —	00	04	02
In 1530, Oats, the Quarter	00	04	00
Beans, the Quarter — --	00	05	04
In 1532, Oats, the Quarter	00	02	08¼
Beans — — —	00	05	04

In 1533, it will not be amifs, to infert a little Piece of Hiftory, out of honeft Mr. *Stow,* to our prefent Purpofe, under this prefent Year.

' It

' It was this Year enacted,
' That Butchers should sell their
' Beef, and Mutton, *by Weight:*
' Beef for a *Half-Penny* the
' Pound, and Mutton for *Three*
' *Farthings:* Which being de-
' vised for the great Commodity
' of the Realm (as it was thought)
' hath proved far otherwise.
' For at that time, *(i. e.* 1533.*)*
' fat *Oxen* were sold for XXVI *s.*
' VIII *d.* fat *Weathers* for III *s.*
' IV *d.* fat *Calves* of the like
' Price. A fat *Lamb* for XII *d.*
' The Butchers of *London* sold
' *Penny Pieces* of Beef, for the
' Relief of the Poor ; every
' Piece two Pound and an half:
' sometimes 3 Pound for a Pen-
' ny. And 13, sometimes 14
' of these Pieces for XII *d.* Mut-
' ton VIII *d.* the Quarter. And
' an 100 Weight of Beef for
' IV *s.* VIII *d.* What Price it
' hath grown to since, it need-
' eth not to be set down. At
' this Time also, and not before,
' were foreign Butchers permit-
' ted to sell their Flesh in *Lea-*
' *den-Hall* Market of *London.*

I suppose by *Foreign* Butchers,
he means such as lived not, or

had

had not ferved their Apprentice-
fhip, in *London*.

	l.	*s.*	*d.*
In 1535, Oats, by the Quarter, at —— —— ——	00	02	08
In 1537, Oats the Quarter	00	03	04
Beans, the Quarter —— --	00	06	00
In 1543, Oats —— —— --	00	03	04
Beans —— —— —— ——	00	06	08
In 1551, Wheat, by the Quarter —— —— —— ——	00	08	00
Malt, at —— —— —— --	00	05	01
Two Quarts of Malmfey ——	00	00	08
Oats the Quarter —— ——	00	08	00
A Load of Straw —— ——	00	05	00
A Load of Coals ——	00	12	00

Whenever you meet with
Coals, in old Accounts, you are
to underftand thereby *Charcoal*,
not *Seacoal*; which has not been
in common (as well as I can
guefs) 150 Years; at leaft not
in *London*: Tho' I find them,
in *M. Paris* under the Name of
Carbo Marinus, in the Time of
H. III. in Additament.

In 1552, Barley, the Quart.	00	05	00
In 1553, Wheat —— ——	00	08	00
Malt —— ——	00	05	00
A Tun of Wine ——	05	00	00
Mufcadel the Quart, at——	00	00	06
Malvefy, the Quart ——	00	00	05
Red Wine the Quart ——	00	00	03

In

	l.	s.	d.
In 1554, Wheat the Quarter, at —— —— —	oo	o8	oo
Rye, the Quarter, at ——	oo	o6	o8
Malt, at —— ——	oo	o5	oo
In 1555, Wheat, the Quarter, at —— —— —	oo	o8	oo
Rye, the Quarter, at ——	oo	16	oo
Malt the Quarter, at —	oo	o5	oo
In 1556, Wheat, the Quart.	oo	o8	oo
Malt, the Quarter ——	oo	o5	oo
Beans, the Quarter — —	oo	o6	o8
In 1557, Wheat, the Quart.	oo	o8	oo
Rye, the Quarter — —	oo	o8	oo
Malt, the Quarter — —	oo	o5	oo
Oats, the Quarter ——	oo	10	oo
For threshing a Quarter of Wheat —— ——	oo	o1	o1
For threshing a Quarter of Rye —— ——	oo	oo	10
For threshing a Quarter of Barley —— ——	oo	oo	o5
Mr. *Stow*, says that in this Year, before Harvest, Wheat was, *per* Quarter —— —	o2	13	o4
Malt, *per* Quarter ——	o2	o4	oo
Beans and Rye, *per* Quarter	o2	oo	oo
Pease, *per* Quarter ——	o2	o6	o8
But after Harvest, Wheat was at *London*, *per* Quarter ——	oo	o5	oo
Malt, *per* Quarter ——	oo	o6	o8
Rye, *per* Quarter ——	oo	o3	o4

But

	l.	*s.*	*d.*
But in the Country Wheat was, *per* Quarter———	oo	o4	oo
Malt, *per* Quarter ———	oo	o4	o8
Rye———————	oo	o2	o8

So that a Penny-Wheat-Loaf, which before Harveft was 11 Ounces, was after Harveft 56 Ounces. My *Private Computus* takes no Notice of thefe *Advances* and *Falls*, to which I return, and fhall only infert, now and then, what Mr. *Stow* fays.

	l.	*s.*	*d.*
In 1558, Wheat the Quarter	oo	o8	oo
Rye———————	oo	o8	oo
Barley ———————	oo	o5	oo
A good Sheep ———	oo	o2	10
In 1559, Wheat———	oo	o8	oo
Rye———————	oo	o8	oo
In 1560, Wheat ———	oo	o3	oo
Rye———————	oo	o8	oo
Barley, at ———	oo	o5	o2
For a Load of old Hay——	oo	12	o6
For a Load of (I fuppofe New) Hay ———	oo	o6	o8
Oats, the Quarter ———	oo	o5	oo
In 1561, Wheat the Quarter	oo	o8	oo
Rye ———————	oo	o8	oo
Malt, the Quarter ———	oo	o5	oo
Oats, the Quarter———	oo	o5	oo
In 1562, Wheat ———	oo	o8	oo
Barley ———————	oo	o5	oo
For a Load of Hay———	oo	13	o4
For a Load of Straw ———	oo	o6	oo

For

	l.	s.	d.
For a Hogſhead of Claret-Wine —————	02	10	00
In 1563, Rye, the Quarter	00	13	04
Oats, the Quarter———	00	05	00

I would not have been weary of tranſcribing ſuch Accounts as theſe, if I had judged the Knowledge of them any thing to your Purpoſe; but I perceive the Way was now, and had been ſo for ſome Years before, as well as many that follow, to ſettle the Price of Corn betwixt the *Landlord* and *Tenant*, without Regard to what it *truly* was. *Wheat* was generally fix'd to 8 *s.* the Quarter, and *Malt* and *Oats* at 5. But finding it ſo for 20, 30, or 40 Years together, you may reaſonably conclude, That was not the true Market-Price, becauſe it is not in the nature of the Thing poſſible, that Corn ſhould be ſo long at the ſame ſtand. But yet if you take Things for 20 Years together, 'tis likely that ſuch a Price might be equal enough, betwixt the Landlord and the Tenant, and therefore well agreed upon. When, therefore, I have given you an Obſervation or two, of Mr. *Stow*'s, relating

to the Publick, I will shut up
this long Chapter, with an Account of the Price of Corn for
these last 60 Years, such as was
indeed the *real* Price, and not
of *Composition* or Agreement; of
which you are to make the best
Use you can, in order to the Satisfaction you require.

In 1574, Such a Dearth at
London, that Wheat was, the
Quarter, at ——————————

Beef (at *Lammas*) so dear,
that a Stone came to ————

And 5 Herrings (so dear)——

Bay Salt (never so dear) the
Bushel sold at ——————

After Harvest Wheat was the
Quarter ——————————
and so continued about a Year.

In 1587, Wheat was, at
London, by the Quarter,——
and in other Places at 10 s. 12 s.
and 13 s. the Bushel. This was
occasioned by excessive Transportation.

In 1594, Wheat, the Quar-
ter, at ——————————

Rye ——————————————

In 1595, Wheat (by much
Transportation) the Quarter, at

A Hen's Egg, at —————

Or, at best, 3 Eggs for ——

l.	s.	d.
02	16	00
00	01	10
00	00	02
00	06	00
01	04	00
03	04	00
02	16	00
02	00	00
02	13	04
00	00	01
00	00	02

A Pound

	l.	*s.*	*d.*
A Pound of fweet Butter —	oo	oo	o7
Our Sins (as Mr. *Stow* fays) deferving it.			
In 1596, Wheat (by reafon of great Rains) the Quarter, at	04	oo	oo
Rye —— ———————	02	o8	oo
Oat-meal, by the Bufhel —	oo	o8	oo
In 1597, Wheat fell from 5 *l.* 4 *s.* the Quarter, to———	04	oo	oo
Rye, from 9 *s.* the Bufhel to 6 *s.* and then to 3 *s.* 2 *d.* and then rofe again to the greateft Price. Bifhop *Goodwin* in his *Annals*, 1557, fays, that in this Year, 1597, Wheat was 13 *s.* 4 *d.* the Bufhel			
In 1598, Pepper fo dear as that a Pound was fold at———	oo	o8	oo
Raifins, at———————	oo	oo	o6
Gafcoign Wine, the Gallon, at ———————————	oo	o2	o8
Sweet-Wine, the Gallon, at	oo	o4	oo

Now

Now follows the Account, I promised you, of the true Market-Price of *Wheat*, and *Malt*, for 60 Years last past.

Years.	Wheat, Qu^r.			Malt, Qu^r.		
1646	02	08	00	01	09	00
47	03	13	08	01	17	00
48	04	05	00	02	00	00
49	04	00	00	02	02	00
1650	03	16	08	01	18	06
51	03	13	04	01	09	00
52	02	09	06	01	08	00
53	01	15	06	01	08	00
54	01	06	00	01	00	08
55	01	13	04	01	00	00
56	02	03	00	01	04	00
57	02	06	08	01	08	04
58	03	05	00	01	09	04
59	03	06	00	02	08	08

Years.	Wheat, Qu.ʳ			Malt, Qu.ʳ		
1660	02	16	06	01	12	08
61	03	10	00	01	13	04
62	03	14	00	02	02	00
63	02	17	00	01	12	08
64	02	00	06	01	10	00
65	02	09	04	01	08	04
66	01	16	00	01	06	00
67	01	16	00	01	02	08
68	02	00	00	01	04	00
69	02	04	04	01	07	04
1670	02	01	08	01	06	06
71	02	02	00	01	05	04
72	02	01	00	01	02	00
73	02	06	08	01	04	00
74	03	08	08	01	14	00
75	03	04	08	01	14	00
76	01	18	00	01	06	00

Years.	Wheat, Qu^r.			Malt, Qu^r.		
1677	02	02	00	01	08	00
78	02	19	00	01	08	08
79	03	00	00	01	06	08
1680	02	05	00	01	02	08
81	02	06	08	01	04	08
82	02	04	00	01	08	00
83	02	00	00	01	08	08
84	02	04	00	01	05	04
85	02	06	08	01	08	00
86	01	14	00	01	05	04
87	01	05	02	01	04	00
88	02	06	00	01	02	00
89	01	10	00	01	00	00
1690	01	14	08	00	19	04
91	01	14	00	00	17	04
92	02	06	08	01	04	04
93	03	07	08	01	10	00

Years.	Wheat, Qu^r.			Malt, Qu^r.		
1694	03	04	00	01	12	00
95	02	13	00	01	12	00
96	03	11	00	01	08	00
97	03	00	00	01	08	00
98	03	08	04	01	12	00
99	03	04	00	01	19	04
1700	02	00	00	01	11	04
1701	01	17	08	01	04	00
1702	01	09	06	01	08	00
1703	01	16	00	01	03	04
1704	02	06	06	01	08	00
1705	01	10	00	01	06	00

In

In this Computation, you are to know, that in every Year there are two Prices of Corn, the one of *Lady-Day*, the other of *Michaelmas*; both which I put together, and take the half, for the common Price of that whole Year. Of the firſt 20 Years of theſe laſt 60, the common Price of Wheat was 2 *l.* 17 *s.* 5 *d.* $\frac{1}{4}$, the Quarter.

Malt was 1 *l.* 12 *s.* 0 *d.* $\frac{3}{4}$, the Quarter.

The common Price of the ſecond Score of Years was,
Wheat at 2 *l.* 6 *s.* 3 *d.* $\frac{3}{4}$, the Quarter.
Malt at 1 *l.* 5 *s.* 3 *d.* $\frac{3}{4}$, the Quarter.

The common Price for theſe laſt 20 Years paſt was,
Wheat at 2 *l.* 5 *s.* 9 *d.* $\frac{3}{4}$, the Quarter.
Malt at 1 *l.* 5 *s.* 5 *d.* $\frac{1}{4}$, the Quarter.

From whence it appears, that, one Year with another, for theſe laſt ſixty, Wheat has been, the Quarter, at —— ——

l.	*s.*	*d.*
02	09	$10\frac{1}{2}$

And

	l.	*s.*	*d.*

And Malt (abating the Fractions) at ——— ——— —

01   07   07¼

Which is, 6 *s.* 2 *d. ob. q.* the Bushel of Wheat, and 3 *s.* 5 *d. q.* the Bushel of Malt, and somewhat above.

Though I ought to acquaint the Reader, that the Market I have computed by, is somewhat higher than those at a very great distance from *London*; in which, if we allow Wheat to have been at 40 *s.* and Malt at 24 *s.* the Quarter, we shall come nearer to the Truth, in general.

C H A P.

CHAP. V.

Of Stipends, Salaries, Wages, Join-tures, Portions, Day-labour, &c.

IN the *Council* held at *Oxford*, 1222, it was decreed, That where the Churches had no greater Revenues than V *Marks per An.* they fhould be conferred on none, but fuch as fhould conftantly refide in Perfon, on the Place. *Spelman, Conc. Angl. Tom.* 2.

A fingle Prieft might therefore fubfift on V *Marks*, but he could not afford to keep a *Curate.*

Accordingly *Ste. Langton*, A. B. *Cant.* in the fame Year decrees, That the *Perpetual Vicar* fhall have V *Marks* affign'd him, *i. e.* as much as may be farmed out for V *Marks*: Except in *Wales*, where by reafon of the Smallnefs of the *Livings* (and Plenty, I fuppofe, of Provi-fions) the Vicars are contented with lefs Stipends. *Ibid.*

In 1287, *Peter Quivil*, B. of *Exon*, *in Synodo Exonienfi*, decrees, That in every *Parochial* Church, the *Perpetual Vicarage* fhould be en-dowed with, at leaft, V *Marks per An.* that he may, in fome Meafure, keep Hofpitality; and in cafe he grow old, fickly, or impotent, may be thereby fuftained. This muft be done, if the Living be really worth XL *Marks per An.*
But

But if it be of better Value, the Vicar's Portion muſt be increaſed.

And as for a *Curate* (whom he here calls *(a)* *Parochialis Sacerdos*) he decrees the *Rector* ſhall pay him 40 *s. per An.* for his Stipend ; and ſays, if the Rectors think themſelves aggrieved by this, they may do their Work themſelves, and ſave that Money. He alſo mentions *Sacerdotes Auxiliarii, (b)* and decrees, that they ſhall have 50 *s. per An.* at leaſt ; and if they have agreed for leſs, *(c)* ſuch Agreement to be void. *Concil. Ang.*

(a) I ſhould have thought, that *Sacerdos* (join'd eſpecially with *Parochialis*) ſhould have ſignified a *Pariſh-Prieſt, Rector,* or *Vicar,* as diſtinguiſh'd from his *Capellanus,* or *Curate* ; but he ſeems to be here, a mere Stipendiary *Curate,* and removeable, whenever the *Rector* will do his Buſineſs himſelf. *(b)* Why an *Auxiliary,* or Aſſiſtant Prieſt, ſhould have 50 *s. per An.* when the *Curate* had but 40, I cannot ſee : But there is very good Reaſon, why ſuch under-hand Bargains *(c)* ſhould be made void, which were ſo much to the Prejudice of poor Curates. And therefore (before this *Conſtitution)* in 1253, among the *Articles of Inquiry,* for all the Dioceſes of *England,* one was, Whether any *Rectors* had made a Bargain with their *Curates,* that beſides the Stipends they received from the *Rectors,* they might receive from others *Annualia & Tricennalia* ; becauſe this permitting of the Curate to be a *Maſs Prieſt,* and to perform *Annualia*

&

& *Tricennalia*, was to fave the Rector from giving fo fair and reafonable a Stipend, as he ought. *Annal. Burton*, in 1253. *Note*, That *Annualia* were fuch Oblations, as were made by the Relations of the Deceafed, upon the Day the Party died, *every Year*: which Day, our Fathers called the *Year's-Day*, or *Year's-Mind*, and, upon it, *Mafs* was celebrated with great Solemnity, by one of the moft confiderable Clergymen, that could be procured, according to the Quality of the Deceafed. *Tricennalia* were called *Trentals*, from *Trigintalia*, and in Englifh, a *Month's-Mind*, becaufe the Service lafted a Month, or 30 Days, in which they faid fo many Maffes. As M. *Du Frefne* obferves on the Word *Tricenarium*, *Officium XXX Miffarum, quod totidem diebus peragitur, pro Defunctis, vel Obventiones quæ obveniunt Sacerdotibus, ratione ejufdem Officii.*

In 1289, *Gilb. Ciceftr.* decrees, The Curates, in poor Churches, muft have V *Marks*, for their Stipend; in richer Churches, they muft have more.

In 1306, *W. Grenefeld*, A. B. *Ebor.* decrees the fame thing. *Concil. Ang.*

In 1308, *Rob. de Winchelfea*, A. B. *Cant.* decrees, That no Curate fhall ferve under V *Marks per An. Idem, ibid.*

In 1348, *H. Knyghton* fays, that the great Peftilence had fwept away fo many Priefts, among other People, that a *Chaplain* could hardly be gotten to ferve a Church, under X *Marks*, or X *Pounds per An.* whereas before, **they**

they might be had at V, or IV *Marks*, nay at II, together with their Diet: and Men would hardly accept of a *Vicarage* of 20 *Marks* or 20 *l. per An.* pag. 2600. This, I suppose, was, because *Vicars* were thought to be obliged to stricter Residence, which, in Pestilential Seasons, was, doubtless, hazardous.

In 1360, *J. Thoresby*, A. B. *York*, decrees the same thing with his Predecessor *Grenefeld* in 1306, *Concil. Ang.* V. 2.

In 1362, *Simon Islip*, A. B. *Cant.* decrees, That Chaplains *Annualia celebrantes*, and having *no Cure of Souls*, shall be content with V *Marks per An.* and they who have *Cure of Souls*, with VI *Marks*, unless the Diocesan, for good Cause, shall order more. But Mr. *Stow* observes upon it, that it occasion'd many of them to turn Robbers, *p.* 265.

The same A. B. the Month after, complains that the Priests grew wanton, and were not content with reasonable Stipends, for serving *Parish Cures*; but went about, rather chusing to say *Masses*, for the Living and the Dead, and get what they could that way, than fix in any certain Place: and therefore orders and appoints the same Salaries above-named; and if any One took any more, under any Pretence whatever, they should be punished. *Concil. Ang.* This had been highly unreasonable, unless V or VI *Marks* had been, at that Time, thought a sufficient Maintenance for a single Person. And so accordingly, about that Time, we find it was the usual Salary.

In

In 1571, *In Stipendiis unius Capellani,* 2 *l.*
13 *s.* 4 *d. Burton Ant. Leiceſt.* 87.

In 1378, *Simon Sudbury,* A. B. *Cant.* re-
peats the Decrees of his Predeceſſor *Simon Iſelip,*
and makes the ſame Complaints. And decrees,
That every ſuch unfix'd *Maſs-Prieſt* ſhould
content himſelf with VII *Marks per An.* either
all in Money; or with Diet and III *Marks* in
Money. And he that takes a *Cure,* to content
himſelf with VIII *Marks,* or with IV. *Marks*
and his Diet. And all this, under Pain of Ex-
communication. *Concil. Angl.*

This Matter ſeem'd to be of ſuch Importance, that the Parliament, in 39 *E.* III. made
Rules about it, in theſe Terms, *c.* 8. ' If any
' Secular Man in the Realm pay any more
' than V *Marks,* to any Prieſt yearly, in Mo-
' ney, or in other Things, to the Value; or
' if he pay to ſuch Prieſt retained to abide at
' his Table, above two Marks for his Gown,
' and his other Neceſſaries, (his Table accounted
' to 40 Shillings) and thereof be attainted, He
' ſhall pay to the King fully as much as he
' paid to the ſaid Prieſt.' And this was renew-
ed in 1414, 2 *H. V. St.* 2. *c.* 2. in the following Manner:

' No yearly Chaplain, within the Realm,
' ſhall take, from henceforth, more for his
' whole Wages, by Year (that is to ſay,
' for his Board, Apparel, and other Neceſſa-
' ries) but VII *Marks.* Nor the Pariſh-Prieſts
' which be, or ſhall be retain'd to ſerve Cures,
' ſhall take, from henceforth, for their whole
                                   ' Wages,

' Wages, by Year (that is to fay, for the
' Things aforefaid) but VIII *Marks:* unlefs it
' be by Licenfe of the Ordinary.   So that the
' whole Sum pafs not IX *Marks.*'   And in
27 *H.* VI. a Pardon was paffed for fuch Priefts
as had offended againft thefe *Acts.*

In 1421, *H. Chichely,* A. B. *Cant.* at the
very importunate Inftance of his Clergy in *Convocation,* does, with the Confent and Advice
of his Suffragans, confirm and ratify the Decree of his Predeceffor, *S. Sudbury,* in 1378,
repeating the very Words of it. *Idem, ibid.*

And in 1439, (which is very near to the
Time you are inquiring after) the fame A. B.
Chichely, in *Convocation* alfo, decrees, That
Vicarages fhall be augmented (by the Rectors,
or Appropriators) to XII *Marks per An.* if the
whole Benefice be worth fo much, to fupport
the Burthens incident to Vicarages. *Id. ibid.*

Vicarages were at firft free from all In-
cumbrances and Burthens; but by the Artifice
of the *Monks,* and *Religious,* the Favour
they found at *Rome,* the Compliance of
the *Bifhops,* and by other Means, they came,
by degrees, to bear almoft equal Charges with
the *Rectors,* though much lefs able to do it.
And therefore, though it was very well, and
wifely done by this Archbifhop to augment
Vicarages to XII *Marks,* yet confidering the
Charges and Burthens incident to Vicarages,
they were not much advantaged by it; for a
Vicarage of XII *Marks,* with its Burthens, may
                                              not

not be so good as a Curacy with VII or VIII *Marks*, without Incumbrance.

And therefore, even in 1439, (which is very near to the Time of the Foundation of your *College)* a single Man was thought to be provided for, by a Stipend of VIII *Marks*, which is but VI *s.* VIII *d.* above the Sum you are inquiring about.   You may therefore very reasonably conclude, that, about that Time, a single Man might live cleanly and decently, with good Management, with V *l. per. An.* because it is not to be presumed, that an *Archbishop*, at the Head of his Clergy, and at their Request too, should decree such an Allowance for officiating Clergymen, as would not keep them (if virtuous Men and sober) decently and cleanly.

Let us see also, a little, to the Allowance of *Chantry Priests*, and such like.

In 1237, *H.* III. gives VIII *l.* out of the Exchequer for 3 Chaplains, to do Duty daily in the *Temple-Church, London*, which is IV *Marks per Ann.* each.   In *Monasticon Anglican.* V. 2. p. 521.

In 1242, *Alexander* B. *Cov.* and *Lichf.* erected an Office of Chanter in that Church, and allowed for his Salary VI *l.* X *s. Ang. Sac.* P. I. p. 446.

In 1313, *E.* II. ordained and commanded, that his Chapel of St. *Edward,* in *the Castle* of *Windsor,* should be kept and served in the Manner following:

1. To

1. To the honour of *God*, of our *Lady*, and Saint *Edward*, for him and his Anceſtors, it is ordain'd there be four Chaplains, who ſhall be Men of good Condition, and diſcreet; of which one ſhall be Head-Chaplain of the Chapel, and the other three ſhall be his Seconds, or Aſſiſtants.

2. Alſo two *Clerks*, of good Condition, and that chant well, and in all Points attendant on the Head-Chaplain, and on the others, as oft as there ſhall be Occaſion for the Service of the Chapel.

3. Each of the aforeſaid Chaplains ſhall ſing Maſs every Day, without ſome good Cauſe to the contrary; ſo that every Morning there be two Maſſes, by *Note*, the one *of our Lady*, the other *of the Day :* the other two *of Requiem*, for the Souls of the Anceſtors of our Lord the King.

4. The Head-Chaplain, to defray his whole Expence, is to receive X *Marks per An.* Each of the other Three an C *s.* the two Clerks, each of them L *s.*

5. And the King's *Chancellor*, whoever he be, becauſe he is the Head of the King's Chapel, ſhall make, once every Year, a Journey thither, if he can be diſpenſed with by the King, to ſee that the ſaid Chapel be ſerved with Ornaments, Library, and Chantry, in the above-appointed Manner; and make out his Breve *de Liberatæ*, for the ſaid Miniſters to be paid their Wages, duly, twice a Year.

6. And

6. And if any of the above-faid fix Chaplains or Clerks fhall die, or be removed, the
faid Chancellor fhall put a fufficient Perfon in his
Place. The Title of this Record is, *De Pro-
videntiis pro Capella Windeforæ:* and it is in
Mr. *Rymer*'s 3d Vol. of *Fædera,* &c.

It appears (5.) that the *Chancellor* was *the
Head of the King's Chapel,* and in the Life of
Thomas Becket (Chancellor to *H.* II.) written
by one who lived at the fame Time with him,
that it was Part of the Chancellor's Office, *ut
Capella Regia illius fit difpofitione & Cura.*
This feems to be the Reafon of the Lord
Chancellor's being (altho' no Clergyman) the
Vifitor of the College of Dean and Canons of
St. *George* in *Windfor-Caftle,* founded by *Ed.*
III. his Son, which is *the King's Free Chapel,*
who was alfo born at that Place, of which
there is this *Memorandum,* in the fame Vol. 3.
1312. which, it will not be much out of my
Way to tranfcribe in this Place.

' *Memorand. Ifabella* the Queen was brought
' to Bed, in *Windfor-Caftle,* on *Monday* the
' next after the Feaft of St. *Martin,* in Winter,
' in the Year of Grace 1312. the 6 *E.* II. of her
' firft-born Son; and in St. *Edward*'s Cha-
' pel in the fame Caftle, he was chriftned
' the *Thurfday* following, by the Cardinal
' *S. Prifca.* His God-fathers were *A. Picta-*
' *vienfis,* Chamberlain to the Pope; *J.* Bp. of
' *Bath and Wells;* *W.* Bp. of *Worcefter;* *Lewis*
' *Count d'Eureux; John* of *Brittany,* Earl of
' *Richmond;*

' *Richmond*; *Aymary de Valence*, E. of *Pembrook*,
' and *Hugh le Despenser*.

In 1315, two Chanters were appointed in
the Church of *Lichfield*, and had, each for his
Salary, V *l*. XV *s*. *Angl. Sac.* P. I.

In 1332, *Elizabeth de Burgh* makes an A-
greement with the *Prior* and *Convent* of *Angle-
sey* in *Cambridgesh*. for XX *l. per Ann*. which
she gives that two Chaplains shall be maintain'd,
with each a convenient *Manse*, or Dwelling-
house, and Diet, and XX *s*. for Robes and
other Necessaries: or else to allow them XII
Marks, to find themselves in all Things; unless the *Prior* and *Convent* can agree with them
for less. And in 1335, she discharges the
Prior and *Convent* of one of those Chaplains,
upon their paying to *Rob. de Spalding*, an Annual Pension of an C *s*. and gives them moreover a Rent-Charge of XI *s*. XI *d*. *Monast*.
Vol. 2. p. 259.

These Chaplains therefore were thought able to
live, each upon VI *Marks*, *i. e.* 4 Pounds *per An*.

Between 1345, and 1381, *Thom*. of *Hat-
field*, B. of *Durham*, founded a *College* for 8
Monks, and 7 young Men, to study the Libe-
ral Sciences; and allowed to each Monk IV *l*.
and to each Student V *Marks*. *Angl. Sacra*.

In 1350, two Priests, to officiate alternate-
ly, during the whole Year, every Day, at the
Church of *Sherifhoton* in the Diocese of *York*;
to pray for the Souls of *R. Nevil*, Ld. *Raby*, &c.
for VII *Marks* between them. In Mr. *Maddox's Formulæ*, p. 450.

In

In 1373, the Master of the Hospital of *Fosse-gate* in *Yorksh.* is to be a Clergyman of good Fame and Discretion; and is to have, for his whole Maintenance, the Sum of X *Marks per Ann.* And if the Revenues increase upon his Management, he is to get another Chaplain to assist him, who, for his Pains, is to have VII *Marks per Ann.* And they must, both of them, constantly *reside*, and constantly *officiate*, on the Place. *Monast.* V. 3. p. 99.

In 1400, *John Plumtree* of *Nottingham*, erected two Chauntries, with two Chaplains to attend daily; to each of whom he allowed C *s.* or V *l. per An. Monast.* V. 2. p. 448.

In 1408, *Fabian* sets it down, that the Stipend of a Mass-Priest was VII *Marks*.

And, not to multiply Instances of this kind, of which you cannot fail of meeting many, in all our Histories; there is a *College* in the *University* of *Cambridge*, founded about the Year 1450, in which the statuteable Allowance to each *Fellow* is V *l. per Ann.* to find him in Diet, Clothes, and all other Necessaries.

You must now be content with *Miscellanies*, the Order of Time however being observed.

Betwixt 871, and 900, King *Alfred* left, by Will, to each of his Daughters, an *Hundred Pounds* in Money. Mr. *Camden* (in his *Remains)* says 400 *l.* But it appears by the *Will*, printed at the end of *Alfred's* Life at *Oxford*, that the 400 *l.* was divided betwixt his 3 Daughters, and one *Alswith:* But the Reader must not think that this was the *whole*

of

of their Portion, for he had fettled *Lands* on each of them before; but this was all he left them in *Money*.

In 1087, when *W. Rufus* came to inquire into the Treafure his Father had laid up at *Winchefter*, he found it by Weight 60000 *l.* of Silver, befides Gold and Jewels. He gave by his Father's Order, and for the Good of his Soul, to each *Great Church (i. e.* Abbey, Convent, or Cathedral) X *Marks.* To each *lefs one* V *Marks*, to every *Parifh Church* V *s.* and to the *Poor* of every *County* an C *l.* Thus *Ingulfus*, who lived at the fame Time.

In 1101, the Compofition betwixt *H.* I. and *Robert* his elder Brother, was, that *Robert* fhould have 3000 *l. per Ann.* in Weight. *Pet. Blæfenf. Contin.* The Words, *in Weight*, are put in, to fignify that the Money fhould not be clipped, for a Pound by *Tale* was at this Time, and long after, moft certainly a Pound *in Weight.*

In 1135, when King *Stephen* was crowned, he feifed the Treafure which *H.* I. had left, which came to 100000 *l.* befides Gold and Silver Veffels, with other Jewels ineftimable. *Tho. Rudborn, Hift. Winton.* p. 284.

In 1193, the Ranfom of *R.* I. was an 100000 *Marks* in Silver. *Rad. de Diceto* fays they were *Pounds.* But Mr. *Rymer*'s Volumes are of greater Authority than any private Writer's Works, being made up of *Records.*

In 1201, K. *John* agreed to pay *Berengaria*, the Dowager Queen of *R.* I. a 1000 *Marks*

per

per Ann. for her Dowry, which he increaſed, in 1215, to a 1000 *Pounds per An.* M. *Rymer, in Anno.*

In 1207, *Amph. Till,* being taken Priſoner by K. *John,* was put to Ranſom at 10000 *Marks,* in part of which he is to pay X Horſes, at the rate of 30 *Marks* a-piece, or in lieu of them 300 *Marks.* Who this Man was, I cannot find, but his Horſes were certainly as high-prized as they could well be.

In 1221, *Joan,* eldeſt Daughter to K. *John,* married to *Alexander* K. of *Scotland,* had a Dowry of 1000 *l. per An. Rymer.*

In 1226, *H.* III. confirms the Dowry of *Iſabella* his Mother, and ſays it was the ſame that *Elianor* his Grandmother had, and makes the ſame to *Elianor* his own Wife, the E. of *Provence*'s Daughter, in 1235, with whom he was to have 20000 *Marks* for Portion. But the *private Inſtructions* were, to accept of 15000, or 10000, or 7000, or 5000, or 3000. Nay, ſhe was to be brought away, tho' they could get nothing at all with her. *Rymer.*

In 1236, *Iſabella,* Siſter to *H.* III. was contracted to the Emperor *Frederic,* with 30000 *Marks. Idem.*

In 1254, *Edward,* the Son of *H.* III. promiſes a Dowry of 1000 *l. per An.* to *Elianor* the K. of *Caſtile*'s Daughter, whilſt he is Prince; but ſays, when ſhe comes to be Queen, he will add 500 *Marks per An.* more. And upon this Marriage, *H.* III. ſettles 15000 *Marks per An.* on the Prince. *Idem.*

In

In 1278, *E.* I. gives, with his Daughter *Joan*, contracted to *Hartman*, Son to the K. of the *Romans*, 10000 *Marks* Sterling; which are to be return'd in case that *Hartman* die before her, together with what Presents the said Husband shall ever make to her. *Idem.*

In 1294, *E.* I. took into his Hands all the Estates of the *Priories-alien*, allowing to every *Monk* 1 s. 6 d. *per Week*, which comes to 3 *l.* 18 s. by the Year. And therefore, I suppose, a Monk might live tolerably well on that Allowance. For the King was not angry with the Monks; but these *Priories* were *Cells* to Monasteries in *France*, (with which Nation the King was now at open War) and whatever Surplusage there was, after the Charges of the *Cells* at home were defray'd, it was sent to the Monasteries or principal Houses abroad; which was indeed feeding the King's Enemies.

In 1299, *Ed.* I. contracts with *Margaret* Daughter to the K. of *France*: 18000 *l. Turonenf.* (four of which make *one* Pound Sterling) being agreed upon for her Dowry. This in English Money came to 4500 *l. per An.* But in 1315, he increased it to 5000 *l. per An. Rymer.*

In 1301, the Widow of *Edmund* E. of *Cornwal* (Son to the K. of the *Romans*, and Nephew to *H.* III.) was, at the Request of several Lords in Parliament, endowed with a Jointure of 500 *l. per An.* by *E.* I. *Tho. Walsingham.*

In

In 1302, *E. I.* promises, to *Isabella* Daughter to the K. of *France*, contracted to his Son *Edward*, 4500 *l. per An. Rymer.*

In 1306, *E. I.* leaves to his Son *Thomas* 10000 *Marks*, to his Son *Edmond* 7000 *Marks, per An.* and to *Elianor* his Daughter, for her Portion, 10000 *Marks*, and 5000 to buy her Apparel. *Idem.*

In 1307, *E.* II. confirms the Grant his Father *E.* I. had made to his Sister *Mary*, a Nun at *Ambrosbury*, of 200 *l. per An.* 40 Oak-Trees for Firing in her Chamber, and 20 *Dolia* (or Hogsheads) of Wine, as long as she continued in the Nunnery, and lived in *England.* And the Reader will not, I believe, be displeased, to see the Care that was taken in those Days, for the Sustentation of the Daughter and the Sister of a King of *England*, in 1313. *Rymer.*

The *King*, to the *Sheriff* of *Wiltes*, greeting.

'FOR as much as We are indebted to our
' deareſt Siſter *Mary*, a *Nun* of *Ambroſ-*
' *bury*, in the Summ of 12 *l.* 7 *s.* 3 *d.* as well
' for Hay, Oats, Litter, and Shooing, as for
' her Servants Wages, whilſt ſhe tarried at
' *Windſor*, in the Month of *December* laſt paſt,
' as alſo for her Expences in travailling from
' *Windſor* to *Ambroſbury*, as in a Bill of our
' *Warderobe*, delivered by our Siſter into our
' Chancery, appears more at large.—We will-
' ing to ſatisfy our Siſter, in this Particular,
' with all the Speed we may, Do hereby com-
' mand you, to pay to our ſaid Siſter, or her
' lawful

' lawful Attorny, the faid Summe, out of the
' Iffues of your Bailifry, without Delay; and
' We, in your Accounts at our Exchecquer,
' fhall make all due Allowance for the fame.

Witneffe, the King, at Windfor,
    Jan. *the* 1*ft*,
                By a Bill of the Warderobe.

In 1309, the Penfions allowed by the King
to the *Cardinals*, and *great Officers* of the *Pope*,
who were, as it were, retained by the Court
of *England*, were, to fome, an 100, but to
moft of them 50 *Marks per An.*

In 1310, *William de Morene* of *Saunford*,
Kt. being taken Prifoner by the *Scots*, had allowed him by *E.* II. for his Wages, 4 *d.* the
Day; and for his Robe, XX *s.* the Year. The
better fort of Prifoners had 3 *d.* ordinary ones
2 *d.* the Day.

In this fame Year, *a Man at Arms* was
allowed 10 *d.* a *Baliftarius* (a Croffe-bow-man)
3 *d.* an Archer or Bow-man, 2 *d.* the Day.
And the Price the King paid for a *Balifta*, was
3 *s.* 8 *d.* Mr. *Rymer*'s *Collections in Annis.*

In 1311, when the Order of *Knights Tem-
plars* was to be deftroyed, their Perfons impri-
foned, and their Eftates confifcated; many of
their Servants, Chaplains, and Dependants,
were, to be fure, utterly deftitute, and undone:
The King, *E.* II. thought himfelf obliged to
make fome Provifion for them. Some of the
Knights were committed to Monafteries, there
                                    to

to do Penance for their Offences; and to them
the King allowed 4 *d.* a Day, which feems to
have been their ufual Allowance, becaufe in
the *Mandate* to the B. of *Bath* and *Wells,* to
make this Allowance to 4 Knights, it is there
faid, *Sicut prius percipere confueverunt.* To
the *Great Mafter, William de la More,* 2 *s.*
To feveral of their *Chaplains,* the King allows
(as the Knights did formerly) 3 *d.* a Day, for
their Diet, and XX *s.* for their Stipend, which
is, by the Year, V *l.* XI *s.* III *d.* To other Servants, 2 *d.* and to inferior ones, 1 *d.* and V, or
X *s.* for their Stipend, or Livery. And for
this, they were to do the fame Service, they
had done to the Knights, whilft the Lands
were in their keeping. *Rymer's Collection.*

In 1314, *Elizab.* Wife of *Rob. Bruce* (King
of *Scotland*) being Prifoner in *England,* is allowed, for herfelf and Family, 20 *s.* by the
Week. To *Rob. Wychard,* Bp. of *Glafgow,*
and *Will. de Lamberton,* Bp. of *St. Andrews,*
Prifoners, is allowed each of them 6 *d.* a Day,
to a *Valet* 3 *d.* to a *Chaplain* 1 *d. ob.* and to
their ordinary Servants 1 *d. ob. Idem.*

In 1316, *Ed.* II. gives to *Theophania,* a
French Lady, a yearly Eftate of 500 *l.* for
ever, becaufe fhe had been *Nurfe* to *Ifabella*
his Queen. *Idem.*

In 1330, *Joan* of *Oxford,* Nurfe to the
Black Prince, had a Penfion of 10 *l. per An.*
and *Maud Plumpton,* a *Rocker,* had 10 *Marks.*
Dr. Kennet, Paroch. Antiq.

In 1326, *Ed.* II. being depofed, had an
100 Marks by the Month allowed to maintain

tain him: which is at the rate of 800 *l. per An. Walfingham.*

In 1495, when the Lady *Anne*, Daughter to *Ed.* IV. and Sifter to Q. *Elizab.* Wife of *H.* VII. was married to *Tho. L. Haward*, eldeft Son to the E. of *Surry*, it was agreed, that fhe fhould be allowed, for her Suftentation, and convenient Diet, of Meat and Drink, 20 *s.* by the Week. And for two Gentlewomen, a Woman Child (*i. e.* a Servant) a Gentleman, a Yoman, and three Grooms, (in all 8 People) 51 *l.* 11 *s.* 8 *d.* by the Year. And for Suftentation of 7 Horfes, 16 *l.* 9 *s.* 4 *d. i. e.* for each Horfe 2 *l.* 7 *s.* ½. M. *Maddox Formul.* p. 109.

In 1091, all the Men of *Croyland*, that will have any Turf out of the *Abbot's Marfh*, muft either work a Day's Work, or give *Three Half-Pence* for one to cut Turves for *Croyland Court. Ingulfus,*

The Serjeant of the Infirmary fhall, for his looking after the Sick, receive for his Reward (if the Party die) a Coat, or 4 *s.* and every one that watched with the Deceafed fhall have 2 *d.* for every Night. *Idem. ibid.*

A Coat is reafonably valued at 4 *s.* but 2 *d.* a Night for watching, was an extraordinary Recompence. This Serjeant of the Infirmary was to have his Livery of Meat, Drink and Bread, and 4 *s. per An.* for Stipend. *Idem.*

In 1225, *Magna Charta*, C. 22. No Sheriff or Baily of ours, fhall take the Horfes and Carts of any Man, for Carriage, except he pay the old Price limited, *i. e.* for Carriage with

2 Horfes

2 Horses 10 *d.* by the Day: and for 3 Horses 14 *d.*

In Antiq. Constitut. Admiralitatis (but of what Age it appears not) it is thus appointed: *Si l' Admiral soit Bacheler, il prendra la jour, pour lui meme, sur la Mer, IV* s. *Si soit Baron, VI* s. *VIII* d. *& s' il soit Count, XIII* s. *IV* d. *Bacheler,* is here a *Knight.* And I guess, as well by the *Language,* as the *Wages,* that this *Constitution* is not very ancient. S. *H. Spelman* in V. *Admiral.*

In 1329, also they shall *harrow* for 3 Days, or shall pay 3 Pence, *i. e.* a Penny for a Day's Work. It must not however, I think, be always concluded, from such Passages as these, that Men worked for a Penny by the Day: because it seems to have been the Custom, in some Places, for some sort of *Holders,* to be obliged to perform such and such Works, for the *Chief Lord,* at such and such a Price. So in the Word *Sesonis,* in S. *H. Spelman's Glossary. Extenta Manerii de Garinges. He is to work a Day's Work every Week, from* Michaelmas *to the First of* August, *and for it he is to receive for each Day,* 3 *Farthings. And from the First of* August *to* Michaelmas, *he is to receive a Penny Half-Penny; excepting the Winter Season. Excepta Sesone hiemali.* See also the Word *Lanceta,* where you will find much such another Custom.

In 1293, the *Parcarii* of the *Earl of Cornwall* were to have 2 Meals, or 2 *d.* by the Day, but the *Earl* would needs have 3 *d.* which the

the Inhabitants complain of. S. *H. Spelman,* in V *Putura.*

I will, in the next Place, give you (out of S. *W. Dugdale's Origines Juridicales)* some Account of the Judges *Fees* or stated *Salaries,* but it is very imperfect, and only better than none at all.

In 1226, The Fee of a Justice was, *per An.* —— ——	X *Marks.*
1239, A Justice of the *Common Pleas* had —— ——	XX *Lib.*
1243, A Baron of the *Exchequer* had —— ——	XL *M.*
And in the same Year, a Bar. of the *Exchequer* had but——	XX *M.*
1259, A Justice of the *King's-Bench* had —— ——	XL *L.*
1260, A Justice of the *Common Pleas* had —— ——	C *M.*
And in the same Year a Just. of the *Common Pleas* had ——	XL *L.*
1262, Chief Justice of the *Common Pleas* had —— —	C *L.*
A Justice of the *Com. Pleas* —	XL *L.*
1265, A Baron of the *Exchequer* had —— —— —	XL *L.*
1269, Chief Justice of the *King's-Bench* had —— —	C *M.*
1281, Chief Justice of the *Common Pleas* had —— ——	XL *L.*
A Just. of the *Com. Pleas* had	XL *M.*

1299, Chief Juftice of the King's-Bench had — —	L *Marks.*
Chief Juftice of the *Common-Pleas* had — — —	C *M.*
Chief Baron of the *Exchequer* had — — —	XL *Lib.*
The Juftices of both *Benches* and Barons of *Exchequer* had each — — —	XX *L.*
1302, A Juftice of the *King's Bench* had — — —	LXXX *M.*
1364, Chief Bar. and the other Barons of *Exch.* had each	XL *L.*
1367, A Juftice of the *Common Pleas* had — — —	XL *L.*
Chief Juftice of *King's Bench* had — — — —	C *M.*
A Juftice of *King's Bench* had	XL *L.*
1382, A Juftice of *Common Pleas* had — —	XL *M.*
1399, Chief Baron of *Exch.* and other Barons had —	XL *M.*
Chief Juftice of *Com. Pl.* had	XL *L.*
A Juftice of *Common Pl.* had	XL *M.*
1402, Chief Juftice of *King's Bench* had — — — —	XL *L.*
1408, A Juftice of *Common Pleas* had — — —	LV *M.*

In 1440, upon a general Complaint of all the *Benches*, and of the *Attorney General*, of the ill Payment of their *Fees*, there was an Inquiry made, what they had ufually received,

for

for the laft ten Years paft, and what the Crown was indebted to them; by which, and by the Anfwer that was made to it, it appears, that the ftanding Fee of each *Chief Juftice* was 40 *l. per An.* but that by private Letters Patent, the *Ch. Juft. of the Com. Pleas* was allowed 180 Marks *per An.* And the *Ch. Juft. of the K. Bench* was allowed 140 Marks *per An.* befides their Fees. And for their *Winter Robes*, 5 *l.* 6 *s.* 11 *d.* ¼. And for *Summer Robes* 3 *l.* 6 *s.* 6 *d.* The Fee of the *Juftices* of both *Benches* was 40 Marks *per An.* their other Allowance was 110 Marks. The Fee of a *Juftice of Affife* was 20 *l.* the Fee of the *Attorney General* was X *l. per An.* and what their other Allowance was, does not appear. The Allowance to the King's *Serjeants*, and the *Attorney*, for Robes, was 1 *l.* 6 *s.* 11 *d.*

In 1545, the *Chief Juft. of the K. Bench* had an Addition of 30 *l.* to his Fee: and each *Juft.* of the fame *Bench*, and of the *C. Pl.* had an Addition of 20 *l.* And indeed, at the very beft, their Rewards feem to have been far from equal to the faithful Difcharge of their moft painful and moft ufeful Office: and yet it hath fo pleafed God to blefs their Labours, that I do not think I mif-reckon, when I fay, That the *Law* hath laid the Foundation of *Two Thirds* of all the *Honours* and *great Eftates* in all *England.*

Let us now fee a little to the Wages of *Workmen* and *Servants*, which has ever been accounted of fuch Importance, that the Parliaments

liaments themfelves have thought fit to take cognizance of it, and to regulate it according to the Rules following; tho', I think, with no great Succefs.

In 1351, Workmen were to take their Wages in *Wheat*, at the Rate of X *d.* the Bufhel, which is 6 *s.* 8 *d.* the Quarter.—— ——

	l.	*s.*	*d.*
Sarclers (that is, Weeders) and Hay-makers, by the Day, ——	oo	oo	oi
Mowing Meadows, 5 *d.* the Acre, or by the Day,	oo	oo	o5
Reapers of Corn, in the firft Week of *Auguſt*, by the Day,	oo	oo	o2
In the fecond Week, and third, and fo on to the End of it, —— —— —— —	oo	oo	o3

Without Meat, Drink, or other Courtefy demanded.

For threfhing a Quarter of Wheat and Rye, —— ——	oo	oo	o2½
For threfhing a Quarter of Barley, Beans, Peafe, and Oats,	oo	oo	oi½
A Mafter-Carpenter, Mafon, or Tyler, by the Day — —	oo	oo	o3
Other Carpenters, Mafons, or Tylers, —— —— ——	oo	oo	o2
Their Servants, or Boys, —	oo	oo	oi½

Plaifterers, Workers of Mud-walls, and their Knaves, or Servants, at the fame Rate, without Meat, or Drink, demanded.

In

	l.	*s.*	*d.*
In 1360, Master-Carpenters,	oo	oo	04
Others, — — —	oo	oo	03
Their Servants, —— ——	oo	oo	02
In 1389, the Bailiff for Husbandry's yearly Wages, together with his Cloathing, once by Year at most, and his Diet, which is supposed in the following Cases:	oo	13	04
The Master Hind, or Chief Husbandman labouring ———	oo	10	oo
The Carter, and the Shepherd, each by the Year ——	oo	10	oo
The Oxherd ——— ——	oo	06	08
The Cowherd ———	oo	06	08
The Swineherd ———	oo	10	oo
A Woman Labourer ———	oo	06	oo
The Dairy-Woman ———	oo	06	oo
The Plough-Driver, at most	oo	07	oo
In 1446, the Wages of a Bailiff of Husbandry ———	01	03	04
His Cloathing (Diet still supposed) -——— ——	oo	05	oo
The chief Carter, and chief Shepherd ———	01	oo	oo
Their Cloathing, each ——	oo	04	oo
A common Servant of Husbandry -——— ——	oo	15	oo
His Cloathing ——— —	oo	03	04
A Woman-Servant —— —	oo	10	oo
Cloathing ——— ——	oo	04	oo
An Infant (*i. e.* one under 14 Years of Age) —— ——	oo	06	oo

Cloathing

	l.	*s.*	*d.*
Cloathing (with Diet) ———	oo	o3	oo

The Servants of Hoſtlers (*i. e.* Innkeepers) Victuallers, and Artificers, at the ſame Rates.

From *Eaſter*, till *Michaelmas*,

A Free-Maſon, or Maſter-Carpenter, with Diet, by the Day——— ——— ———	oo	oo	o4
Without Diet ——— ———	oo	oo	o5½

A Maſter-Tyler, Slater, Rough-Maſon, a mean Carpenter, and other Artificers, building

by the Day, with Diet —	oo	oo	o3
Without Diet ———	oo	oo	o4½
Other Labourers, with Diet, 2 *d.* without Diet ——— ———	oo	oo	o3½

From *Michaelmas* to *Eaſter* they had a Penny by the Day leſs, the Days being then ſhorter.

But in time of Harveſt a

Mower had, with Diet———	oo	oo	o4
Without Diet ——— ——	oo	oo	o6
A Reaper, and Carter, with Diet, 3 *d.* without Diet———	oo	oo	o5
A Woman Labourer, and other Labourers, with Diet —	oo	oo	o2½
Without Diet, by the Day—	oo	oo	o4½
In 1514, a Bailiff of Huſbandry's yearly Wages——— ———	o1	o6	o8
His Cloathing (Diet ſuppoſed)	oo	o5	oo

Chief

	l.	*s.*	*d.*
Chief Hind, Carter, and Shepherd, each ———— ——	01	00	00
Cloathing (with Diet) ——	00	05	00
Common Servant of Husbandry ———— ——— ——	00	16	08
Cloathing ———— ————	00	04	00
Women Servants yearly Wages ———— ——— ——	00	10	00
Cloathing ———— ————	00	04	00
A Child *(i. e.* a Servant) within 14 Years of Age ———— ——	00	06	08
Cloathing ———— ——— ——	00	04	00
From *Easter* to *Michaelmas,* the daily Wages of			
A Free Mason, with Diet, 4 *d.* without Diet was ——— ——	00	00	06
A Master Carpenter, with Diet, 4 *d.* without Diet was —	00	00	06
A Rough Mason, with Diet, 4 *d.* without Diet was ————	00	00	06
A Bricklayer, with Diet, 4 *d.* without Diet was ———— ——	00	00	06
A Tyler, with Diet, 4 *d.* without Diet was ———— ——	00	00	06
A Plummer, with Diet, 4 *d.* without Diet was ———— ——	00	00	06
A Glazier, with Diet, 4 *d.* without Diet was ———— ——	00	00	06
A Carver, with Diet, 4 *d.* without Diet was ———— ——	00	00	06
A Joiner, with Diet, 4 *d.* without Diet was ———— ——	00	00	06
From *Michaelmas* to *Easter,* with Diet, 3 *d.* without Diet——	00	00	05

A Ship-

A Shipwright's Wages was from *Candlemas* to *Michaelmas*,

1. A Mafter Carpenter, with Diet, 5 d. without Diet———	oo	oo	07
2. A Hewer, with Diet 4 d. without Diet ———————	oo	oo	06
3. An able Clincher, with Diet 3 d. without Diet ———	oo	oo	05
4. A Holder, with Diet, 2 d. without Diet —————	oo	oo	04
5. A Mafter Calker, with Diet, 4 d. without Diet———	oo	oo	06
6. A mean Calker, with Diet, 3 d. without Diet—————	oo	oo	05
A Calker labouring by the Tide, with Diet —————	oo	oo	04

From *Michaelmas* to *Candlemas*, their Wages were,

	With Diet,	Without Diet,
	d.	*d.*
1.	4	6
2.	3	5
3.	$2\frac{1}{2}$	$4\frac{1}{2}$
4.	$1\frac{1}{2}$	3
5.	3	5
6.	$2\frac{1}{2}$	$4\frac{1}{2}$

Other Labourers, from *Eafter* to *Michaelmas*, except in Harveft-time, had by the Day allowed, with Diet, 2 d. without it ——————— | oo | oo | 04 |

From

	l.	*s.*	*d.*
From *Michaelmas* to *Easter*, with Diet, 1 *d.* ½, without it—	00	00	03
In Harvest-time, a Mower, with Diet, 4 *d.* without it——	00	00	06
A Reaper, and a Carter, with Diet, 3 *d.* without it ———	00	00	05
A Woman Labourer and other Labourers, with Diet, 2 *d.* ½, without it —————	00	00	04½

The Reader is not to think that these Rules were every where observed; but no Body could *demand*, or *sue* (I suppose) for greater Wages, than were here allowed : and yet the different Cheapness or Dearness of Provisions in several Countries, must be allowed to make amends for different Wages; and therefore these Rules could not be universally reasonable.

C H A P.

CHAP. VI.

The Conclusion.

TO apply the Chapter of *Corn*, and make it useful to your present Purpose, you must, in the first place, remember, that, during the whole Reign of *Henry* VI. excepting the first and last Years of it (which contains 17 Years above the Time of your Enquiry, which is from 1440 to 1460,) there were XXX *s.* in the Pound; whereas there are *now* (and have been for above an 100 Years) LXII *s.* The Ounce of Silver was *then* at II *s.* 6 *d.* 'tis *now* at V *s.* II *d.* So that the V *l.* (which is the Sum you are concerned about) did *then* contain 40 Ounces; and V *l. now,* does not contain above 19 Ounces $\frac{1}{3}$. From whence you may safely conclude, that V *l.* in the Reign of *H.* VI. was of somewhat better Value, than X *l.* now-a-days is. In the next place, to know somewhat more distinctly whereabouts an E-quivalent to your ancient V *l.* will come, you are (as I before hinted) to observe how much Corn, Meat, Drink, or Cloth, might have been purchased 250 Years ago, with V *l.* and to see how much of the modern Money will be requisite to purchase the same Quantity of Corn, Meat, Drink, or Cloth, now-a-days. To this End, you must neither take a very dear Year, to your Prejudice, nor a very cheap one,

one, in your own Favour; nor indeed any fingle Year, to be your Rule; but you muft take the Price of every particular Commodity, for as many Years as you can (20, if you have them) and put them all together; and then find out the common Price; and afterwards take the fame Courfe with the Price of Things, for thefe laft 20 Years; and fee what Proportion they will bear to one another; for that Proportion is to be your Rule and Guide.

Thus, if for 20 Years together (from 1440, to 1460,) the common Price of *Wheat* were VI s. VIII d. the Quarter; and if from 1686, to 1706, the common Price of *Wheat* were 40 s. the Quarter; 'tis plain that V l. in H. VI. Time, would have purchafed 15 Quarters of Wheat; for which you muft have paid, for thefe laft 20 Years, 30 Pound. So that 30 Pound *now*, would be no more than equivalent to V l. in the Reign of H. VI. Thus if *Oats*, from 1440, to 1460, were generally at 2 s. the Quarter, and from 1686 to 1706, were at 12 s. the Quarter, 'tis manifeft that 12 s. *now*, would be no more than equivalent to 2 s. *then*, which is but a fixth Part of it. Thus if Beans were *then* 5 s. and *now* 30 s. the Quarter, the fame Proportion would be found betwixt 5 l. and 30 l. But you muft not expect that every Thing will anfwer thus exactly. *Ale*, for Inftance, was, during the Time of your Founder, at Three-half-pence the Gallon; but it has been, ever fince you were born, at 8 d. at the leaft: which is but 5 times more, and

a little

a little over.   So that 5 *l.* heretofore (betwixt
1440, and 1460,) would purchase no more
Ale, than somewhat above 25 *l.* would *now.*
Again, good *Cloth*, such as was to serve the
best *Doctor* in your *University*, for his Gown,
was (between 1440, and 1460,) at 3 *s.* 7 *d. ob.*
the Yard; at which Rate, V *l.* would have
purchased 27 Yards, or thereabouts.   *Now,*
you may purchase that Quantity of fine Cloth,
at somewhat less, I think, than 25 *l.*   So that
25 *l. now,* would be an Equivalent to your 5 *l.*
then, 250 Years since, if you pay about 18 *s.*
the Yard, for your Cloth.   I think I have good
Reason to believe, that Beef, Mutton, Bacon,
and other common Provisions of Life, were six
times as cheap in *H.* VI. Reign, as they have
been, for these last 20 Years.   And therefore
I can see no Cause, why 28, or 30 *l. per An.*
should *now* be accounted a greater Estate, than
V *l.* was heretofore, betwixt 1440, and 1460.

Sir *H. Spelman* (a very competent Judge and
Estimator of these Matters) complains, That
the Laws have not sufficient Regard to the different Price of Things, when they condemn People
to death, for stealing Things to the Value of *twelve*
Pence; for tho' that is according to Law, yet that
Law was made when *twelve Pence* would have
purchased as much as you must now-a-days give
20, 30, nay 40 *s.* for.   And he instances in a
Quarter of Wheat, which in the *Assise of Bread,*
51 *H* III. was rated at *twelve Pence*, but, in
his Time, was often sold for 40 *s.* and upwards.
Tis certain, the Laws do never condemn any
One

One to death, for ftealing to the Value of *one*,
no, nor *three*, or *four* Shillings: But 'tis certain
that many die for ftealing Things of lefs Value
than 20 *Shillings*. And therefore, I think, I
have very fufficient Reafon (not to *determine*,
but) to *conjecture*, that 5 *l*. 260 Years ago, was
equivalent to 28, or 30 *l*. now. And confequently, that he who has *an Eftate of Inheritance*, or *a perpetual Penfion*, of that Value,
now-a-days, may as honeftly hold a *Fellowfhip*
with it, as he, who lived 260 Years ago, might
have held it, with 99 *s. per Ann*. Nor does my
Kindnefs and Concern for you, biafs my Judge-
ment in this Affair; for I have thought the
fame Thing, long before your Queftion was
put; and, indeed, ever fince I could confider
the Difference of Times, and the different
Prices of Corn and all other Commodities. And
I had rather put your Confcience on this Bot-
tom, whofe Reafon is clear, and founded upon
Matter of Fact, and Hiftory not to be con-
troul'd; than upon the common Prefumption,
that your Founder did certainly intend, *his Scholars* fhould live like *other Scholars* of the Univerfity; and that the Way of living being *now*
much changed (do not offer to fay improved)
from what it was fo long ago, you muft needs
be at liberty to live in the fame Manner; for I
dare fay, that neither your Founder, nor any
other Founder, if he were now alive, would
admit of many expenfive Articles, which the
corrupt Cuftoms of the Times, and multitude
of Examples, have made young People think
necelfary;

neceffary; and which, I am perfuaded, muft
fome time or other be reformed, as Things neither
ufeful nor creditable to the Life of a Student.
But of this, you will think I have faid at leaft
enough.

The Application of the Chapter of *Stipends*
to your Purpofe is this; That if, about your
Founder's Time, 7 or 8 Marks was judged a competent Provifion for a fingle Clergyman, and 8
Marks do not much exceed 5 *l.* then V *l.* was a
tolerable Maintenance for a fingle Student. And
if fo, then if 28, or 30 *l.* be now-a-days but a
fufficient Maintenance for a fingle Student (fo-
ber and virtuous) it can be prefumed to be
no more *now*, than 7 or 8 Marks *heretofore*
was, and therefore may be enjoyed with the
fame Innocence and Honefty, together with a
Fellowfhip, according to the Founder's Will.

I have now difcharged my Engagement, and
given fuch Anfwer to your Queftion, as I think
is reafonable and honeft; and might here
take my leave of you, if I did not think it
would be acceptable enough, both to you and
other Readers, to acquaint you, that fince I
was employed in writing an Anfwer to your
Queftion, I had another put to me, concerning the *Oath* which the *Sheriff* of a County
puts to fuch as are *Electors* of Parliament-Men,
if he thinks fit; *viz.* Whether they have
Lands or Tenements to the yearly Value of
40 *s. ultra Reprifas?* *i.e.* Whether they have
40 *s. per Ann. clear*; all certain and neceffary
Charges being abated and deducted: for tho' a
Man

Man may receive 8 *l.* a Year for his Eftate,
yet if his *Quit-Rent*, or any other certain Payment, be 13 *s.* 4 *d.* that Man has not an Eftate
of 8 *l. ultra Reprifas*, becaufe there is 13 *s.* 4 *d.*
to be reprifed, or *taken back again*, which is,
I think, the Meaning of the Word. Now this
Act of Parliament was made, 8 *H.* VI. when
40 *s. per Ann.* clear of all Incumbrance, was at
leaft equal to 8 *l. per Ann.* now-a-days. (I put it
fo low to avoid all Cavil and Difpute.) When
a Freeholder therefore, does *now* take his Oath,
that he has an Eftate of 40 *s. per Ann.* 'tis manifeft he does not mean 40 *s.* as it was valued
when that Act of Parliament was made (1430,)
but as 40 *s.* go *now* (in 1706.) Is it not therefore manifeft, that he does not fwear to the Purpofe and Intention of the Law-givers, and only
fwears true to the *Denomination* of 40 *s. per Annum?* To this I anfwered, That doubtlefs the
Purpofe and Intention of the Legiflators, in
1430, was defeated by fuch an Oath, when he
who fwears has really but 40 *s. per Ann.* as
Money and Things go *now.* But yet that fuch
an Oath was honeftly taken, and without any
perjurious Fraud, or Refervation, becaufe taken
according to the literal Senfe of the Words of
it, and becaufe taken in the Senfe of thofe who
adminifter it, and (as is moft reafonably prefumed, tho' not declared) in the Senfe of the
Legiflative Power, which accepts, and juftifies
fuch Proceedings, and which has equal Power
and Authority, to put what Signification it
pleafes on Words, with the Parliament that
made

made that Act, in 1430. These Things, when put together, may look, at first sight, somewhat odly; that *one* Man may swear he is not worth V *l. per Ann.* according to the Statute that requires such Oath, when he is really worth more than X, or XX *l. per Ann.* and *another* may swear he is worth 40 *s. per Ann.* when he is really not worth 10 *s. per Ann.* according to the Statute that first imposed that Oath. You see then how necessary it is to distinguish Times.

Whether the Legislative Power, in 1430, did well, and wisely, in reducing the Number of Electors to such as were worth 40 *s. per Annum*, (which cut off many hundred thousand Voices, and consequently many Occasions of Tumults and Disorders) is not to be doubted overmuch; nor yet is to be over-confidently affirmed, because if it had been so wise and useful an Ordinance, it would have still been kept up, in its due Proportion, according to the Difference of Times; altho' the Changes of such Moment are not to be frequently and lightly made. But in these Affairs, it is not fit for private People to meddle.

I have but one Thing more to offer to your Consideration, from the Accounts I have given of the different Price of Corn, and other Commodities, and then I will put an end to this long Letter: And that is, That if ever you design to take Orders, and obtain any *Rectory, Vicarage,* or higher *Dignity* in the Church, you be, above all Things, careful, how you make

any

any Compofition or Agreement, for any long
Space of Years, to receive a certain Price of
Money, for the Corn that is due to you, altho'
for the prefent it may feem a tempting Bargain, and a profitable Exchange, and rid you
of fome Trouble. You know not what Time
may bring forth, nor what great Alterations
may happen, nor what great Mifchiefs you, un-
wittingly, may do your Succeffors. But I cannot better reprefent my Meaning, nor fhew you
the ill Confequence of fuch Agreements, than
in the Words of Dr. *Kennet*, in his *Parochial
Antiquities*; out of which, I will, with his
Leave, and for your Sake, and for the common Benefit, tranfcribe a Page or two, to our
prefent Purpofe, *p.* 604. ' For the Mifchief of
' a dead and unimproved Allowance in *Money*,
' there is a good Inftance cited in a Charter to
' the Church of *Peterborough* (fee *Gunton*'s *Hift.*
' put out with great Additions by Bp. *Patrick*)
' by *Walter de St. Edmundo* about 1240, where
' the Abbot does grant, for God's Sake, and in
' refpect to Peace, that inftead of the Affize
' for Corn, which the *Cellerarius* paid him out
' of *Belaffife*, he would hereafter accept of an
' Equivalent in Money, *viz.* for 28 Quarter
' and one Schepe (*i.e.* a Bufhel) of Wheat, he
' fhould receive IV *l.* XIII *s.* IX *d.* by which
' Computation each Quarter was then valued
' at 3 *s.* 4 *d.* Had the Abbey continued, what
' an unhappy Bargain had it proved by this
' Time, when the Rent muft have kept
' ftanding at 4 *l.* 13 *s.* 9 *d.* whereas the prefent
' Value

' Value of the Corn would have been feldom
' lefs than *Fifty Pounds*. Such like Prejudice
' was done to the Church of *Sulthorn* (now
' *Souldern*) *Com. Oxon.* the Rector whereof ufed
' to receive from the Abbot and Convent of
' *Ofeney*, one Acre of Bread-Corn, growing on
' their Demefne of *Mixbury*, and four Pence
' from their Demefne of *Fulewell*, till about the
' latter End of *Hen.* III. *Robert de Hay*, Rector
' of that Church, agreed to receive One hun-
' dred Shillings from the faid Abbey, to pur-
' chafe to himfelf and Succeffors, the Annual
' Rent of *five Shillings*, in full Compenfation
' for the faid Acre of Corn. So when *Maud*
' *de Chefny* had given to the Prior and Canons
' of *Burcefter* 5 Quarters of Bread-Corn, out
' of her Manor of *Heyford* (now *Heyford*
' *Warine*) *Com. Oxon.* to be delivered yearly to
' them, on Condition they fhould find Hofts,
' or confecrated Bread, at the faid Church of
' *Heyford*; when this Manor and Church were
' conveyed to *New College in Oxf. Tho. Ban-*
' *bury* (Prior of *Burcefter*) and his Convent did,
' in 2 *H.* VII. *Ann.* 1486, releafe the faid Rent-
' Charge of Corn, for the Confideration of *fix*
' *Shillings and eight Pence*, yearly in Money;
' which, by this Time, would have borne no
' greater Proportion to that Quantity of Wheat,
' than 1 does to 30. When Parifh-Churches
' were firft appropriated to Religious Houfes,
' they were fupplied by fecular Priefts, who
' were ftipendiary Curates, with the Salary of
' V, or at beft, but X Marks; and when by
' the

‘ the Ordination of Vicarages, the Stipend was
‘ exchanged into a ſtanding Portion of Tithe
‘ and Glebe, and Manſe, ſuch Endowment
‘ was generally proportioned to the Pecuniary
‘ Rate of V or X Marks; ſo that the Al-
‘ teration at that Time, was no Benefit to
‘ the Prieſt, only as it better’d his Title,
‘ and made him a perpetual Vicar, inſtead of
‘ an Arbitrary Curate. But conſider, if the
‘ Portion of the Vicar had been allotted in ſuch
‘ a certain Sum of Money, what Mendicants
‘ muſt our Country-Vicars *now* have been!
‘ Whereas the Aſſignation being made in im-
‘ proveable Land and Tithes, by this Means
‘ (the Value of Money abating, and the Rate
‘ of Land and Commodities advancing) ſome
‘ Vicarages, which at the firſt Ordination had
‘ no greater Endowment than what was equi-
‘ valent to V Marks, do *now* afford the Main-
‘ tenance of 50 *l. per. Ann.* Hence the Me-
‘ mory of Sir *Thomas Smith* is highly to be
‘ honoured, for promoting the Act in 18 *Eliz.*
‘ whereby it was provided, That a third Part
‘ of the Rent upon Leaſes made by Colleges,
‘ ſhould be reſerved in Corn, payable either in
‘ Kind or Money, after the Rate of the beſt
‘ Prices in *Oxford* or *Cambridge* Markets, on
‘ the next Market-Day before *Michaelmas* and
‘ *Lady-Day.* This worthy Knight is ſaid to
‘ have been engaged in this Service, by the
‘ Advice of Mr. *Henry Robinſon,* ſoon after
‘ *Provoſt* of *Queen's-College, Oxon.* and from
‘ that Station advanced to the See of *Carliſle.*
‘ And

' And Tradition goes, that the Bill paffed the
' Houfes, before they were fenfible of the
' good Confequences of it. We know, in
' the latter Times of our Confufion, a Project
' was carried on, of deftroying the ancient
' Right of Tithes, and converting that pious
' Maintenance of the Clergy into fettled Por-
' tions of Money. How fatal this Innovation
' would have been in Time, is ingenioufly
' urged by two ingenious and learned Writers,
' (Mr. *Stephens*'s Preface to Sir *H. Spelman* of
' Tithes; and Dr. *Comber*, Hiftor. Vindication
' of Tithes, *p. 2. c.* 10.) We have had fome
' Benefices in *England*, altered by fuch Me-
' thod by Decrees in *Chancery*, with a certain
' Sum in Money, allotted in Compenfation of
' all Tithes: This may feem an Eafe, and
' perhaps an Advantage, upon the firft Eftab-
' lifhment of it. But, unlefs the Incumbent
' be invefted with a Power of Revocation;
' and, as the Reafon alters, can affume his Right
' of Tithing, I am fure, in an Age or two,
' the Succeffors will fuffer extremely by fuch
' a Bargain. For a Living now, of *one hun-*
' *dred Pounds per Annum*, in Compofition-Mo-
' ney, will, in a future Generation, by the
' ftinted Revenue, not exceed another Living
' that is not, at prefent, of half the Value in
' Glebe and Tithe. And it will then (too late)
' appear, that the Predeceffor, who complied
' with fuch a Change, did not confult the In-
' tereft of the Church; and that fuch a De-
' cree did not become a *Court of Equity*. It
                                          ' is

' is very obvious to confider, That nothing
' has been a more unjuft Diminution of fmall
' Tithes, than the Cuftom of a Rate *in Money*,
' inftead of the titheable Thing in Kind; tho'
' fuch Rate, no Doubt, when firft impofed,
' was equivalent to the Things remitted for
' it, whereas they now bear but fmall, or no
' Proportion to it. As for Inftance, in one
' of the old *Saxon* Laws (confirmed by the
' *Conqueror*) it is provided, That if a Man
' have one or two *Colts*, he fhall pay for the
' Fall of each *one Penny*, and the like for
' *Calves*; which was a juft Proportion, when
' the beft Colt or Calf was not valued above
' 10 d. But the Iniquity is, that this Cuftom
' does *ftill* obtain in many Parifhes; and the
' like minute Confideration, for *Wool* and
' *Lambs*, where, for Cuftom Sake, the Tithe
' muft be taken, without any Allowance for
' the much advanced Value of them; by which
' Means, the *Modus Decimandi* is a growing
' Injury, and calls for a Relief by Law, when
' it fhall pleafe the Wifdom and the Juftice of
' our Governors. Thofe eight Men of Qua-
' lity and Learning, who were appointed, at
' the Beginning of the Reformation, to col-
' lect fuch Ecclefiaftical Canons, as ought to
' remain in Force, did freely declare their
' Judgment, *That* thefe Cuftoms ought to be
' abrogated. And the learned Dr. *Cowell* has
' profeffed the fame Opinion, that it is reafon-
' able to take away all fuch Cuftoms, as do
' leffen the Tenth Part, due to the Church of
' God. (The *Interpreter* in the Word *Tithes*.")
Thus

Thus far that learned and experienced Perfon, to whofe Authority I can add nothing, fince what he fays is plain, reafonable, and confirmed by Matter of Fact. And I do heartily concur with him, in wifhing the Gentlemen of the Clergy would ferioufly confider thefe Matters, whenever they have Occafion. And thus you fee, that the Confideration of thefe fmall Matters may be of Ufe, in Things of great Importance. I have only to add, That I fhall think myfelf well paid for my Pains, if I have given you the Satisfaction you defire, and any little Encouragement to look yourfelf into the *Antiquities* of your Native Country, according to the very laudable Example of many excellent Perfons of your *Famous Univerfity*.

I N D E X.

I N D E X.

INDEX.

T. Oſborne *gives Notice, that he now ſells the under-mentioned Book for* 2 *Guineas bound and gilt, which was formerly ſold for* 2 l. 15 s.

A
SURVEY

OF THE
CATHEDRALS

OF

York, Durham, Carlisle, Chester, Man, Litchfield, Hereford, Worcester, Gloucester, Bristol, Lincoln, Ely, Oxford, Peterborough, Canterbury, Rochester, London, Winchester, Chichester, Norwich, Salisbury, Wells, Exeter, St. Davids, Landaff, Bangor, *and St.* Asaph.

Containing an Hiſtory of their

Foundations, Builders, Ancient Monuments, and Inſcriptions; Endowments, Alienations, Sales of Lands, Patronages;

Dates of Conſecration, Admiſſion, Preferment, Deaths, Burials, and Epitaphs of the Bishops, Deans, Precentors, Chancellors, Treasurers, Subdeans, Archdeacons, and Prebendaries, in every Stall belonging to them:

With an exact Account

Of all the *Churches* and *Chapels* in each *Dioceſe*; diſtinguiſhed under their proper *Archdeaconries* and *Deanries*; to what Saints dedicated, who *Patrons* of them, and to what Religious Houſes *appropriated*.

The whole extracted from numerous Collections out of the *Regiſters* of every particular *See, Old Wills, Records* in the *Tower,* and *Rolls* Chapel.

And illuſtrated with Thirty-two curious Draughts of the *Ichnographies, Uprights,* and other Proſpects of theſe *Cathedrals*; newly taken, to rectify the erroneous Repreſentations of them in the *Monaſticon,* and other Authors.

In Three Volumes.

By Browne Willis, *Eſq;*

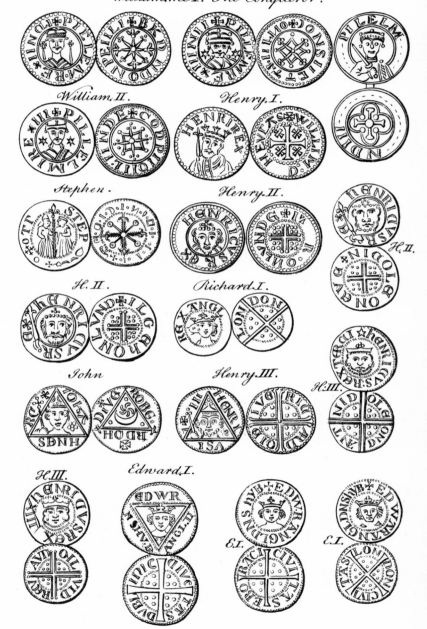

English Silver Coins Plate I.

William the I. The Conqueror.

William II.   Henry I.

Stephen.   Henry II.   H. II.

H. II.   Richard I.   H. III.

John   Henry III.   H. III.

H. III.   Edward I.   E. I.   E. I.

Plate II.

Edward. III. Penny.

Richard. II. Penny.

Half Penny. H. IV.

Henry. V. Groat.

Edward. IV. Groat.

Henry. VII. Groat.

mifplaced

E. III. Groat.

Henry. IV. Groat.

H. VI. Groat.

R. III. Groat.

Plate. III.

Henry. VIII. Teston.

Broadfaced Shilling.

Edward. VI. Shilling.

Crown
E. VI.

Mary. I. Shilling.

Ed: VI. Shilling.

Philip & Mary's Shilling.

Elizabeth's. Crown.

Plate IV.

2. Eliz. Sovereign (in Gold) misplaced

2. Eliz: two Pence

2. Elizabeths. Crown.

James I. Penny

2. Eliz: Groat.

Charles I. Shilling

James I. Shilling

Charles I. Shilling.

Charles I. Shilling.

Charles I. 2 Pence.

Charles I. Groat.

Plate.V.

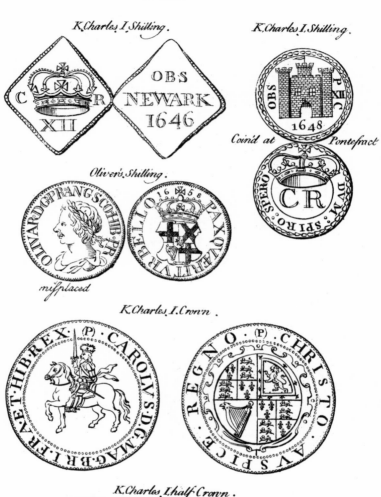

K.Charles I. Shilling.

OBS
NEWARK
1646

C R
XII

K.Charles I. Shilling.

OBS
1648

Coin'd at   Pontefract

SPERO DVM SPIRO

CR

Oliver's Shilling.

OLIVAR D G RP ANG SCO HIB &c

16 58 PAX QVÆRITVR BELLO

XII

misplaced

K.Charles I. Crown.

· CAROLVS · D · G · MAG · BRI · FR · ET · HIB · REX · (P) ·

· CHRISTO · AVSPICE · REGNO · (P) ·

K.Charles I. half Crown.

· CAROLVS · D · G · MAG · BRI · FR · ET · HIB · REX · (P) ·

· CHRISTO · AVSPICE · REGNO · (P) ·

Plate.VI.

K.Charles.I.Sixpence.

The Commonwealth's Crown.

Commonwealth's Shilling.

Commonwealth's Sixpence.

AN
APPENDIX

TO

Chronicon Preciosum:

CONTAINING

An Historical Account of COINS:

In General,

Of the *Original* of COINS ; by whom Money was
first coined ; and to whom the *Privilege* and
Prerogative of Coining, *&c.* properly belongs :

In Particular,

Of the *Standard,* and the several *Alterations* which
the COIN of *England* has undergone ; as also the
Names and Description of the COINS, in Copper-
Plate, from *WILLIAM the Conqueror* to the
Restoration.

LONDON:

Printed for T. OSBORNE, in *Gray's-Inn.*

M.DCC.XLV.

A N
Hiſtorical Account
O F
C O I N S.

C H A P I.

Of the Original of Coins. *By whom Money
was* firſt *coined, and to whom the* Privilege
and Prerogative *of Coining, &c.* properly
belongs.

IT is not neceſſary for me to trace the original Cauſe of Money; but, I ſay, after that
Money was found to be the Commenſurate Bal-
lance, and its intrinſick Value and Eſtimate by
common Conſent was allowed and agreed upon
to be the only convenient and valuable Compenſation in all manner of Commerce, Bargains and
Contracts; to prevent Frauds and Abuſes in de-
baſing the Valuation of the precious Metals of
Gold and Silver, it was, as is moſt probable, uni-
verſally or generally agreed and thought moſt fit,
That Kings, Princes and States, who are natu-
rally intruſted with the Lives, Liberties and Eſtates
of private Perſons, ſhould be alſo intruſted with
the Mint, or the ſtamping, coining, and ſetting
the Eſtimation, Denomination, Price and Value
of Gold and Silver Money: For, as every King,
Prince, or ſupreme Governor of any State, ought
to be the *Pater Patriæ*, or to take the ſame Care
for the Good of his Subjects, as a Father doth for
the Welfare and Honour of his Children and Family; ſo it was conceived that they were the moſt
proper and fit Perſons to be confided in about this
weighty and univerſal Concern of putting and
eſtabliſhing the Denomination, Value and Cur-
rentneſs upon Money; who, as it was hoped,
would diſtribute Juſtice impartially and equally to
every individual Perſon within their Dominions,
and under their Subjection and Allegiance.

Hence

a In his *Dia-tribæ* of Money, p. 35.

Hence it is that *Leigh* obferves,[a]That the Coin-ing of Money is a fpecial Right and Prerogative of Sovereign Majefty, of which the *Roman* Princes did not a little glory ; and according to *Hales*[b] it

b See his Trea-tife concerning Sheriffs Accts, cap. I. p. 2, 3.

is the inherent Regality and Prerogative of the Crown of *England*, and pertains to the King alone, to fettle the Currentnefs, Allay, Weight, Deno-mination and intrinfick Value, and to eftablifh a Price to the Quantity, and to put a Stamp or Im-preffion on it ; which being done, the Coin be-comes current for fo much as the King hath li-

c See *Plowden* Com. fol. 136. *Davis* Rep. fol. 19. *Coke*'s 2 Inft. 576.

mited it fhall pafs for,[c]

That the Kings of this Nation do juftly claim this Prerogative from ancient Ufe, does appear by the many notorious Changes of Money made in the Times of our feveral Kings and Queens fince the *Norman* Conqueft, as hereafter fhall be fhewn. For though feveral Acts of Parliament have paffed concerning Exchanges and the Exportation of *En-glifh* Moneys, and the Importation and Utterance of foreign, and bafe, or falfe Money ; fo there are alfo feveral Ordinances of the Kings of *England*, made without the Confent and Advice of Parlia-ment, called (in this Cafe) *Statutes* ; viz. *Statutum de Moneta magnum*, and *Statutum de Moneta par-vum* ; which are alfo called and adjudged to be Statutes ; becaufe the Ordinance of the King with a Proclamation in fuch Cafes has the Form of an Act of Parliament. And

As this Preheminence is a Part of the King's Regality and Prerogative, fo it is a Part of his

d See Sir *Matt. Hales*, ib.

regal Revenue,[d] which is called the King's *Seig-niorage* or *Royalty*, or *Coinage* ; for in every Pound Weight of Gold, the King had commonly five Shillings for his Coinage, out of which he gene-rally allowed twelve Pence, but fometimes eigh-teen Pence to the Mafter of the *Mint* for his Work and Trouble : and upon every Pound Weight of Silver the *Seigniorage* or *Coinage*, anfwered to the King in the Reign of *Edward* the *Third*, was eight Penny-weights *Pondere* ; which, according to Sir *Matthew Hales* was equivalent to one Shilling, out of which the King allowed fometimes three Parts in four to the Mint Mafter, referving only the
fourth

fourth Part to himſelf. But in the Reign of
Henry the *Fifth*, the King's *Seigniorage* of every
Pound Weight of Silver was fifteen Pence.[e]

e See Rot. Parl.
9 *Hen.*V. part 2.
n. 15.

Altho' the Authorization, Denomination and
Stamp of Coin, was undoubtedly the Right of
the Kings of this Nation ; yet our ancient *Saxon*
Kings communicated this Prerogative to their
Subjects.[f] Then we find that in every good Town
there was a Coiner, but in *London* there were eight,
and at *Canterbury* ſeven, *viz.* four on the King's
Account, two for the Archbiſhop, and one for the
Abbot ; at *Winchester* ſix ; at *Rochester* three ; at
Hastings two, and the ſame at *Hampton*, *Exeter*,
Shaftsbury, *Lewes*, and *Chichester*.[g] And, as *Ro-*
ger Haywood obſerves, this Prerogative of the
Crown was uſurped even after the Conqueſt by the
Barons: For in the Civil Wars in King *Stephen*'s
Time, about the Year 1149, and the 14th Year of
that King's Reign, *Omnes Potentes, tam Episcopi*
quam Comites et Barones, ſuam faciebant Monetam,
i. e. *All the great Men of the Realm, as well the*
Bishops as the Earls and Barons, coin'd their own
Money. But as ſoon as *Henry* the *Second* found
himſelf peaceably and ſecurely fixed on the Throne,
he put an End to this Uſurpation of the Baronage,
Novam fecit Monetam, quæ ſola recepta erat et ac-
cepta in Regno, i. e. *He coin'd new Money, and or-*
dain'd that it only ſhould paſs current within this
Kingdom and received in Payment. From which
Time the Exerciſe as well as the Right of coining
Money in this Kingdom has remained in the
Crown without Interruption : For tho' the Crown
by diverſe Charters, Grants and Privileges, yielded
to ſeveral of the ancient Biſhopricks, Abbeys, &c.
a Power to erect a Mint within their own Juriſ-
dictions, and there to coin their own Money ; as
the Abbot of *St. Edmond's-Bury*, the Biſhop of
Durham, Archbiſhop of *York*, &c.[h] they had neither the Denomination, Stamp nor Allay, but only
the Profit of the Coinage : For whenever the King
thought proper to change the Coin by his royal
Proclamation, he at the ſame Time iſſued out a
Mandate to the Treaſurer and Barons of the Exchequer to deliver a proper Stamp to thoſe private
Mints, to be thenceforward uſed by them in Coining, during his royal Pleaſure. But this Liberty

f See *Camden*'s
Rem. Title
Money.

g See *Hales*, ib.
p. 4, 5.

h See *Stow*'s
Annals, p. 284.

of

of Coinage in private Mints, being attended with many Impofitions, Loffes and Hardfhips on the trading Part of the Nation, hath, according to my Lord Chief Juftice *Hale*, been long fince dif-ufed, and in a great Meafure, if not altogether, re-affumed by the Statute of 3 *Henry* VII. cap. 6.

The Advantage of a current Coin is thus ob-ferved by the ingenious Mr. *Lock* ;[i] *In coined Silver or Money*, fays he, *there are three Things which are wanting in other Silver* ; *as*, Firft, *Pieces exactly of the fame Weight and Finenefs.* Secondly, *A Stamp fet on the Pieces by the public Authority of the Coun-try* ; *and*, Thirdly, *A known Denomination given to thefe Pieces by the fame Authority.* Befides, coined Silver Money differs from uncoined Silver in this, *viz.* That the Quantity of Silver in each Piece of Money is afcertain'd by the Stamp it bears; for the Stamp is a Mark, and, as it were, a public Voucher, that fuch a Piece, of fuch a Denomina-tion, is of fuch a real Weight and Finenefs, or has fo much pure Silver in it ; which precife Weight and Finenefs, by Law appropriated to the Piece of each Denomination, is called the *Standard.*

i See his Confid. conc. the Rai-fing the Value of Money, p. 5. & 22.

The Matter or Species whereof the current Coin of this Kingdom hath been made, has been conftantly (at leaft fince the Days of King Henry I. and II.) Gold and Silver allay'd with Copper ; tho', as Sir *Matthew Hale* [k] obferves, in ancient Times, the Species, whereof the Coin was made, might poffibly be pure Gold or Silver ; and this Allay, fays he, was that which gave the Denomi-nation of *Sterling* to our Coin, *viz. Sterling* Gold and *Sterling* Silver, and is the Standard of Fine-nefs for our Money here in *England:* and I think this natural Account of the Antiquity of the Word *Sterling* among us, tho' Antiquarians are fo divi-ded about it, [l] may ferve to convince every rea-fonable Enquirer, that this Term in our Coinage is to be carried as far backward as *Henry* I. or at leaft to the Reign of *Henry* II. As to its Deriva-tion, I refer you to the learned and ingenious Au-thor, of *Nummi Britannici Hiftoria.*[m]

k Ib. cap. I. p.5.

l See *Nummi Britan. Hiftoria,* printed *Anno* 1726, p. 3, 4.

m Pag. 2,3,4,5.

Having

Having thus ſhewn to whom the Prerogative of Coinage belongs, I ſhall now proceed to ſhew, which of the *Roman* Emperors and *Britiſh* Princes in this Nation were the firſt that impreſſed or ſtamp'd their own Image on their Coins.

It is obſerved by ſome Authors, [n] that *Julius Cæſar* was the firſt that had his own Face ſtampt on the *Roman* Coins, and that *Conſtantine* the *Great*, Emperor of *Conſtantinople*, firſt engraved the Croſs upon his Coin; a Uſage that has been generally obſerved by all his Succeſſors, and other Chriſtian States. And it has been likewiſe obſerved, [o] that *Cunobeline*, Prince and Ruler of the *Trinobantes*, the greateſt and moſt potent State of the ancient *Britains*, for the greater Honour of his State, was the firſt of this Nation, that cauſed his own Image to be ſtampt on his Coin, after the Manner of the *Romans*, who had a little before done the ſame Thing in Honour to *Julius Cæſar*. Before this, the *Britains* are recorded to make all their Payments with Rings of Iron and Plates of Braſs, aſſized at a certain Weight; ſome of which *Speed* avoucheth that he himſelf had ſeen dug out of the Earth, and found in little Cruſes or Pitchers of Earth. [p] This Prince *Cunobeline* reſided at *Camalodunum*, now called *Malden*, in *Eſſex*, as appears by the Reverſe of his Coins, and was Son of *Theomantius*, Nephew to *Caſibelan*, Prince of the *Trinobantes*, and General of all the *Britains* in their Wars againſt *Cæſar*.

n See *Speed's* Chron. printed 1633, fol. 25. and *Leigh's* *Diatr.* of Money, p. 35.

o See *Speed's* Chron. p. 31, 32, 53. Edit. ead.

p See *Speed's* Chron. p. 31, 32, 48, 53. and *Stow's* Annals, p. 23.

After this, the other *Britains* beginning to traffick with diverſe Nations, by means of the *Romans*; they followed their Example in the civiliſed Method of ſtamping Silver and Gold Money with the Faces of their Princes, after the Example of *Cunobeline*. [q] Some of theſe Coins are ſtill extant in the Collections of the Curious, and are known to be *Britiſh* from their particular Forms, being commonly emboſſed outward, and Shield like, on which the Inſcription or Face is ſeen, with a hollow Reverſe, within which is ſet their Device; a Form uſed by no other Nation, except among ſome of the *Grecians*.

q See *Speed*, ib. p. 25, 181. and *Nichol.* Engl. Hiſt. lib. 1. c. 3.

Thus

Thus the Coins of this Iſland multiplied according to the Number of its independent Princes, till the *Romans*, having conquered the whole Realm, and extinguiſhed or (at leaſt) reduced the Kings thereof under their Power and Tribute, ſuppreſſed the *Britiſh* Coins alſo, ſupplying their Place with their own Coin, as a Proof of their Conqueſt and Subjection to the *Roman* Yoak. This Change may properly be dated from the Reign of the Emperor *Claudius*, from whoſe Time the *Roman* Coins only were current in *Britain*, for three hundred Years, at leaſt till the Reign of *Valentinian* the Younger ; tho' Mr. *Camden* computes this Currency to have continued five hundred Years : [r] During which Time, tho' all the Money for this Part of the World, under the *Roman* Government, was for the moſt Part coin'd either at *Rome*, *Lyons*, or *Triers*, yet the Emperor *Conſtantine the Great* diſtinguiſhed *London* with the Honour of a Mint during his own Reign ; and Mr. *Camden* aſſures us, that he had ſeen ſome Copper Coin of that Date with this Inſcription, *P. London. S.* viz. *Pecunia Londini Signata* ; which is alſo confirmed by the Officer under the Emperor, ſtiled *Præpoſitus Theſaurorum Auguſtantium*, viz. *The Treaſurer of the Mint at* LONDON ; for, *London*, that now is, was called *Auguſta* in the Declining State of the Empire. Of which *Roman* Coins many have been and are ſtill found in the Ruins of ancient Towns and Caſtles, which were hid, as ſome probably conjecture, when *Maximus* carried ſo many *Britains* into *France* with him, or when the *Saxons* and other Northern Invaders over-ran this Iſland, and deſtroyed the ancient Habitations, as well as their Inhabitants.

r See his Rem. Title *Money*.

The *Romans* at laſt, not willing to maintain their *Britiſh* Conqueſt at ſo dear a Rate, as to be obliged to keep a continual Armament againſt the *Picts* and *Scots*, &c. who were always plundering their Borders, left the *Britains* at their own Liberty, and independent on the *Roman* State ; but had ſo ſtored the Nation with their Coin, that, it is probable, it continued the only current Coin to the Year 561, or thereabouts ; for none of our Antiquarians ever ſaw any Coin of the *Britiſh* Princes *Vortigern*, *Vortimer*, *Conſtantine*, *Aurelius Conanus*, *Vortiporus*,

Vortiporus, Aurelius Ambroſius, Arthur, and others, who lived in thoſe ancient Times. As for the *Britains* or *Welch,* whatſoever *Jura Majeſtatis* or Royal Prerogative their Princes had, they never had any Coin of their own, ſays *Camden.*[r] Therefore,

r See his Rem. Title *Money.* See alſo *Nicholſ.* Eng. Hiſt.Lib.I.

Both he and *Speed* in his 7th Book affirm, that the moſt ancient *Engliſh* Coin upon Record is that of *Ethelbert,* the fifth King of *Kent,* as I ſaid above, about the Year of our Lord 561, Monarch of the *Anglo-Saxons,* and firſt *Chriſtian* King, except you will admit *Lucius* of our *Engliſh* Nation.

cap. 3.

This is he that ſet an Example to his Succeſſors in the Monarchy; for after him ſeveral of the *Anglo-Saxon* Monarchs, *viz. Offa, Kenwolfe, Egbert, Elfred, Edward* the Elder, *Edmund, Edwin, Edgar, Edward* the Martyr, *Etheldred* and *Edmund* Ironſide had their Coins[s] with their proper Devices. And

s See *Speed's* Chron. book 7.

Now People firſt began to account their Money by *Pence, Shillings, Pounds,* and *Mancuſes.* The *Pence,* (which is properly derived from the *Latin* Word *pendo* to weigh, on Account of the exact Weight thereof)weighing about three Pence of our preſent Money, were rudely ſtampt with the Monarch or King's Image on one Side, and with the Mint Maſter's on the other, or elſe with the Name of the City where it was coined.

This Method continued after the Conqueſt for ſome Time, only with this Contrivance, of a Croſs ſo deeply impreſſed, that it might be eaſily broken and divided into two Halfs or four Quarters; each Half ſo broken received the Name of an *Halfpence* or *Half-penny;* and each Quarter ſo divided received the Name of a *Fourthing* or *Farthing:* From whence you have the proper Derivation of our preſent Half-penny and Farthing.

Five of theſe *Saxon* Pence made their *Scillinge* or *Shilling,* ſo called by them from the Roman *Scilingus,* or fourth Part of an Ounce. Eight and forty of theſe Scillinges made their Pound, which anſwered to our Pound *Troy,* or twelve Ounces.[t] Their

t See *Cam.*Rem. Title *Money.*

Their *Mancus* contained thirty of thoſe Pence, and is by ſome ſuppoſed to be the ſame Denomination as a *Mark* or *Marca*; becauſe *Camden* obſerves, that he had found *Manca* and *Mancuſa* tranſlated *Marca* in an old Book. They are thought to have had both Gold and Silver Pieces of this Denomination of Money; for the *Kentiſh* Men are recorded to purchaſe their Peace of *Ina* King of the Weſt *Saxons* at the Price of 30,000 *Mancuſes* of Gold. But in the Notes upon the Laws of *Canutus,* we are to obſerve that *Mancuſa* ſignifies no more than a Mark of *Silver*, or a *little Mark*, whereas *Manca* was a Square Piece of Gold commonly valued at *thirty Pence.*

u See *Cam.*Rem. Title *Money.*

After the *Saxons* were overpowered by the *Danes,* the Conquerors introduced a new Reckoning [u] of Money by *Ores* or *Oras*, as may be ſeen in Dooms-day Book. As no ſuch Piece has been preſerved by Poſterity, it is uncertain whether this was a diſtinct Coin or a certain Sum; yet it is accounted that twenty *Oræ* made two Marks of Silver, according to the Abbey Book of *Burton*; and I can't help thinking that the Sound of *Denmark,* called *Ore* Sound, where Ships pay Toll (*viz.* ſuch a Number of *Oræ*) hath its Name from theſe *Oræ.*

As to the Gold Coin of this Nation, we find none older than the Reign of *Edward* III. Tho' we read of a certain Gold Coin called a *Bizantine* or *Bizant*, current here long before; ſo called from *Conſtantinople,* anciently called *Bizantium,* and not from being coined at *Beſanſon* in *Burgundy,* as ſome Frenchified Antiquarians have dreamt. The Value of this Coin is now quite forgotten, yet I can't but obſerve that the Name ſtill continues in the *Blazon* of Arms, where Plates of Gold are called *Bizants.* And thoſe great Medals or Pieces of Gold, which the King of *England* offereth upon High Feſtival Days, ſays our learned *Camden,* of the Value of about 15 Pounds, are ſtill called *Bizautines.*

x See *Nummi Britan. Hiſt.* p. 22, *&c.*

To conclude this Chapter, the Pieces which King *Edward* III. firſt coined in Gold were called *Florens* or *Florences*, becauſe *Florentines* were the Coiners thereof.[x]

CHAP.

CHAP. II.

Of Sterling *Money.*

A S to the antiquated Diſpute about the Derivation of the Term *Sterling,* which is an
old Term or Epitheton of Money current and le-
gally coined in this Nation,* I ſhall only refer you
to the *Nummi Britannici Hiſtoria.* ʸ

*See before,p.6.

y Page 2, *&c.*

This Money has been always accounted of ſo
pure an Allay, that it has at all Times been the
moſt fixed and unalterable Standard of Money in
all the known World, to the great Encouragement
of Commerce, and Honour of our Nation: The
Money Standard of other Nations having been
found very uncertain and variable.

Nor do I pretend to fix the certain Time when
this Name of *Sterling* Money was firſt uſed a-
mong us; this is equally as difficult as to clear the
Uncertainty of its Derivation: Yet it is certain,
that this Name was in Uſe in the Reign of *Henry*
III. and King *Edward* I. but it can't be ſuppoſed
to be as old as the Conqueſt, becauſe, as my Lord
Hale remarks, it is not to be found in Dooms-
day Book, where there is ſo great an Occaſion of
mentioning Rents, Payments, *&c.*

This Epithet *Sterling* was in ancient Times
added to Money, to denote as much as what we
now call *bona et legalis Moneta Angliæ,* or, *good
and lawful Money of England,* whether in Gold or
Silver; to which ſix Things muſt concur to make
it current and lawful Money: Firſt, Weight, ſe-
condly, *Fineneſs;* thirdly, Impreſſion; fourthly,
Name; fifthly, the Authority of the Prince; and
ſixthly, Proclamation.　For every Piece ought to
have a certain Proportion of Weight or Poize, and
a certain Proportion of Purity or Fineneſs,which is
called Allay or Alloy; and every Piece does as
neceſſarily require a certain Form of Impreſſion
which ſhall be known to all Men: For as Wax is
not a Seal without an Impreſſion of ſome Sort
upon it, neither is a Piece of Metal, Money, without

out a proper Denominative Stamp or Impreſſion ;
and alſo every Piece of Money muſt have or take
its Name from its Value, or from what it is ordained by the Prince to paſs in Payment for, ſuch as
a *Penny,* a *Groat,* a *Six-pence, Shilling, Half-
Crown, Crown, Half-Guinea, Guinea,* &c. And
all this ought to be done and fixed, by the Authority and Commandment of the Prince, for
otherwiſe the Money is not lawful; neither is it
then current, till publiſhed by the Proclamation of
the Prince.

All theſe Circumſtances are as ancient as Money itſelf in all civiliſed and well governed States,
and do appear in the ancient Orders made by the
Kings of *England* for the Coinage of Moneys,
which are repoſited in the Tower of *London* for
this Realm of *England,* and in the Caſtle of *Dub-
lin* for the Kingdom of *Ireland:* As alſo in the
Indentures between the King and Miniſters or Officers of the Mint for the Time being; for they always contain the Proportion of Weight, Fineneſs
and Allay, with the Impreſſion, Inſcription, Name
and Value of the Moneys to be coined.

As the Coinage of Money is a Flower and Prerogative of the Crown of great Antiquity ; ſo the
counterfeiting, clipping, fileing and defacing the
Coin of this Realm, has been of a long ſtanding
and continued Practice. In the 27 *Henry* II.
which is above five hundred and ſixty Years ago,
the Money was ſo abuſed and corrupted, that he
found it neceſſary to call it in, to be changed for
new Money then to be coined. — About 25 Years
after, *viz. Anno* 1205, King *John* obſerving that
the Abuſe of Money was either in a great Part
continued or revived, called it in again, and cauſed
it to be new coined; and thereby brought it to a
greater Purity or Fineneſs than it had been before in
any of his Predeceſſors Reigns: On which Account, ſome Authors fix upon him as the Inventer
or firſt Ordainer of Sterling Money. About 42
Years after this Coinage by King *John,* King
Henry III. *Anno* 1247, finding the current Coin
ſo clipped and abuſed, called it in by Proclamation ;[y]
in which among other Things, ſays my Author,
is this laconick Reflection upon the *Jews, Circum-
cidebatur*

cidebatur à circumciſis Judæis, becauſe the Money was clipped or *circumciſed by the circumciſed Jews;* or *Italian* Uſurers, then called *Corſini,* (who were the firſt *Chriſtians* that brought in Uſury among us [z]) and the *Flemings.* — Again about the Year 1278, and the ſeventh Year of *Edward* the *firſt,* the ſaid Prince called in the Money, and eſtabliſhed a certain Standard for *Engliſh* Coin, appointing and ordaining a Sterling Penny to weigh, the 20th Part of an Ounce; and cauſed two hundred and eighty *Jews* to be hanged for clipping his Coin.[a]   And about twenty one Years after this, in the Year 1299, the ſaid King commanded that the *Crocards* and *Pollards,* (two of which made one Sterling Penny) the *Roſaries, Staldings, Eagles, Leonines, Mitres* and *Steepings,* being white Moneys, artificially made of Silver, Copper and Sulphur, ſhould be cried down and prohibited; and inſtead thereof were coined other new Moneys and *Half-Pence* of *Silver;*[b] which Ordinance was alſo tranſ-mitted and ſent over into *Ireland,* and enrolled in the Red Book of the Exchequer there.[c]— The ſame good Example of watching and rectifying the corrupted Coin of his Realm was, about thirty-ſeven Years after, followed by King *Edward* III. in the ninth Year of his Reign, *A. D.* 1334, who not only called in the baſe Money, but coined new Forms or Pieces, by the Name of *Groats,* of four Pence Value, and *Half-Groats,* of no more than two Pence, equivalent to the *Sterling* Money,[d] at the ſame Time forbidding the Utterance of *black* Money made of Copper, as *Mail* and *Black Mail,*[e] upon Pain of the Forfeiture thereof.

z See Bp. *Fleet-wood*'s Sermon againſt clipping, fol. 17, 18.

a *Walſingham* Hypod. Neuſtr. p. 69.

b See *Baker*'s Chron. fol. 101

c See *Davis*'s Rep. fol. 20. *Hales*'s Treatiſe conc.Sher. cap.I. p. 20. and Lib. Rub.Scac.pars 2. fol. 2, 6.

d See *Baker*'s Chron. fol. 128.

e *Camd.* Rem. Title *Money.*

In the Year 1409, and 2 *Hen.* IV. the Par-liament prohibited the Uſe of *Gally-half-pence,* a Sort of Money imported by the *Gallies* of *Genoa,* which Republick at that Time carried on a great Trade with *England,* and by that Means intro-duced their baſe Money among their Cuſtomers; and the King in 1411 ordered new Money to be coined.[f]

f Idem, ib.

In the next Reign, 3 *Henry* V. and *A. D.* 1414, the baſe Money called *Suſkins* and *Doitkins* under-went the ſame Fate with the *Gally-half-pence* by the ſame Authority :[g] And here Mr. *Blount*[h] ob-ſerves, and *Doitkin.*

g See *Coke*'s 3 Inſt. fol. 92.

h In his *Nomo-lexicon,*verb. *Gally-half-pence,*

ſerves, that it is from this prohibited baſe Coin of ſmall Value, a *Doitkin*, that we ſtill retain the Phraſe, *not worth a Doitkin*, when we would energetically expreſs the Meanneſs or little Value of any Thing.

This ſame King, after his Victory at *Agincourt*, and Peace with *France*, ordered a ſilver Coin to be ſtruck with this Stile or Inſcription, *Rex Angliæ*, *Regens et Hæres Franciæ*, i. e. *King of England, Regent and Heir of France*. A Gold Coin called a *Salus* or *Salute* of the Allay of Sterling, Value twenty-two Shillings, with the Angel ſaluting the Virgin *Mary* on one Side, the one holding the Arms of *England*, and the other the Arms of *France*, with the King's Titles ; and *Chriſtus vincit, Chriſtus ſignat, Chriſtus imperat*, on the Reverſe. But in the next Reign, or 2 *Henry* VI. this Silver Coin, which was called a *Blanch*, or white Money, to diſtinguiſh it from the *Salus*, or yellow Money, coined at the ſame Time in *France*, being found not to be of the Allay of Sterling, was alſo prohibited [i] by Order of the Parliament in 1423.

i See *Blount's* Nomolexicon in ver. *Blanks. Stow's* Annals fol. 586. *Camd.* Rem. Title *Money.*

After this we find that baſe Money, which from Time to Time found a Circulation thro' the Corruption of the Times, and other Accidents, was called in about the Year 1464, or in the 5 *Edward* IV. *Anno* 1503, in the 19 *Henry* VII. *Anno* 1544, in the 36 *Henry* VIII. *Anno* 1550, or the 5 *Edward* VI. But never effectually till Queen *Elizabeth*, in the Year of our Lord 1559, and the ſecond of glorious Reign, who cried down and prohibited all mixed and baſe Money, and eſtabliſhed a new Standard of pure Sterling, which continues to this Day. Yet,

All this could not prevent the Iniquity of After-Times : For during the unnatural Civil Wars and Rebellion againſt King *Charles* I. the *Engliſh* Coin ſuffered ſo much by clipping, filing and ſniping, that the Keepers of the Liberties of *England* (as the Murderers of the ſaid King choſe to call themſelves, by Authority of their pretended Parliament) were obliged to call it in ; and ordained that all the new Money, thence forward to be coined, ſhould, inſtead of the King's Effigies and Impreſſion,

Impreffion, and his Title, Arms and Superfcription, have on one Side thereof a St. *George*'s Crofs ftamped with thefe Words circumfcribed, *The Common-wealth of England,* and on the other Side of the Coin, *the Crofs* and *Harp*, with this Motto, *God with us* : And this remained a current Coin till the Reftoration of King *Charles* II. tho' *Oliver* was no fooner fixed in his Protectorfhip, than he endeavoured to ennoble and perpetuate his Name by a filver Coin, with his Head laureat a-la-Romaine, *Olivar. D. G. A P. Ang. Scot. Hib.* &c. *Prot.* on the Reverfe, a Shield with the Imperial Crown of *England,* St. *George*'s Crofs in the firft and fourth Quarters, St. *Andrew*'s in the fecond, the *Irifh* Harp in the third, and his Paternal Arms, *viz.* a Lion Rampant in an Efcutcheon of Pretence, Legend. *Pax quæritur Bello,* 1658. And his Crown Piece was circumfcribed on the Rim with thefe Words, *Has nifi periturus mihi adimat nemo.*

King *Charles* II. being reftored, immediately prohibited the Currency of the late rebellious Coin, and ordered a new Coinage, which Money had the King's Buft on the one Side, with his Title and his Arms and Motto on the other Side.   But this new Coin being only performed after the old Fafhion by Stamps and Hammers, was ftill liable to the pernicious Practice of clipping, filing, *&c.* in fo much that before three Years were ended, this new Money was fo diminifhed in its Value, that in 572 Bags of one hundred Pounds each, which ought to have weighed in all 221,418 *oz.* 16 *dwts.* 8 *gr. Troy,* yielded no more than 113,771 *oz.* 5 *dwt. Troy*; fo that in thefe 572 Bags there was a Deficiency of 107,647 *oz.* 11 *dwt.* 8 *gr. Troy,* occafioned by the Money being clipped; and confequently the Money being reduced to lefs than one half of its intrinfick Value.[k]   In the Year 1663, it was found neceffary, for remedying this Lofs to the Nation, to call in all the light and bad Money, and to fupply it with a new milled Coin,[l] which Money was firft fabricated on the twenty-fourth Day of *December* 1663 : And from hence we may date the Beauty of our *Englifh* Coin; tho' the defperate Fortunes of fome, and the evil Inclinations of others, have ftill found Means to counterfeit, and clip, *&c.* the current Money.   King

[k] See *Lowndes's* Effay.

[l] See *Nummi Britan. Hiftor.* p. 112, *&c.*

King *William* III. perceiving this growing Miſchief, called in all the bad Money, and took ſuch
Meaſures with his Parliament as wholly to deſtroy
and extirpate this wicked Practice; as we at this
Day, being 48 Years after, do joyfully expe-
rience.

C H A P. III.

Of the Coins ſince the Reign of WILLIAM
the Conqueror *to this Time.*

THE Word *Coin* has been much tortured
in the Way of Grammatical Criticks for an
Etymology: But, to omit the many conjectural
Derivations thereof, I am inclined to adhere to the
Opinion of Sir *Edward Cooke*,[m] who ſays that the
Word *Coin* is derived from χοινὸς, id eſt *communis*,
quod ſit *omnibus rebus communis* ; becauſe it is *commonly* made uſe of in all Affairs; for as Money is
the Sinews and Strength of a State, ſo it is the
Life and Soul of Commerce; the Mean for all
Commodities, and anſwereth all Things. Thus
when the Value of any Thing is expreſſed, it is
ſaid to be worth ſo many Pence, Shillings or
Pounds; ſo that Money is a Change or Pawn for
the Value of all other Things, and therefore Coin
is properly derived from χοινὸς.

m See *Cooke* on
Litt. fol.207. b.

The Workers of Coin are called *Moneyers*,[n] as I
apprehend, from the Latin *Monetarii* ; and is the
common Name of all the Officers of the Mint,
which make, coin and deliver out the King's
Money. And, as Mr. *Lock* obſerves, there were
paid ſixteen Pence halfpenny for coining a Pound
Weight of Silver, or five Pence halfpenny for
every twenty Shillings, till the Year 1696, when it
was enacted that the Charge of making new
Money of Silver proceeding from clipt Monies
ſhould not exceed fourteen Pence upon every Pound
Weight Troy, or four Pence and the third Part of
two Pence, for every twenty Shillings over and
above the Charges of melting and refining the
ſame. And here, as a Bill of the Mint-Maſter's
Accounts ſhews not only the Charge, but the diſtinct Charge of every Part in the Coinage, I preſume, it will be admitted as a Piece of Curioſity
to inſert the following Account. *Viz.*

n See *Regiſter,*
fol. 262.

The

The Account of Sir *Robert Harley*, Knight of the *Bath*, Maſter and Worker of his Majeſty's Monies within the Mint in the Tower of *London*, from the laſt Day of *March* 1648, to the 15th of *May* 1649 included, being one whole Year, one Month, and fifteen Days, as follows.

	l.	*s.*	*d.*
Inprimis, The ſaid Accomptant chargeth himſelf with Arrearages due upon the Foot of his Account ending the laſt of *March* 1648, as by the ſaid Account appeareth, the Sum of ———	01	13	02
Item, For Monies received for the Workmanſhip of 5 *cwt.* 3 *lb.* 2 *oz.* 12 *dwt.* 12 *gr.* of Crown Gold Monies, at 6 *s.* 5 *d. per lb.* the Sum of——	161	09	00
Item, For the Workmanſhip of 10 *cwt.* 53 *lb.* 11 *oz.* 10 *dwt.* of Silver Monies, at 14 *d. per lb.* the Sum of———————	61	09	07½

Sum total of the Charge is £224　11　09½

Whereof

	l.	*s.*	*d.*			
Paid to the Moneyers for making the ſaid Crown Gold Monies, at 2 *s.* 5 *d. per lb.* ———	60	16	01	95	18	08¼
Item, Paid to them for making of the ſaid Siver Monies at 8 *d. per lb.*	35	02	07½			
Item, paid to Sir *John Wcollaſton* for melting of 5 *cwt.* 3 *qr.* 19 *lb.* 23 *gr.* of Crown Gold Bullion Scizel and Allay, at 6 *d. per lb.* —	14	19	06			
Item, Paid to him for melting of 11 *cwt.* 11 *lb.* 10 *oz.* 11 *dwt.* 12 *gr.* of Silver Bullion Scizel and Allay, at 2 *d. per lb.* ——————	10	01	10			
Item, Paid to him for 26 *lb.* 8 *oz.* 6 *dwt.* 13 *gr.* of Copper Allay, at 16 *d. per lb.* ————	01	15	06	33	16	04
Item, Paid to him for 12 *oz.* of fine Silver to make Gold Aſſays with, at 5 *s.* 9 *d. per oz.*———	03	09	00			
Item, Paid to him for 10 *lb.* 1 *oz.* of Aquafortis, uſed alſo for Aſſays, at 6 *s. per lb.* ————	03	00	06			
Item, Paid to him for Gold-melting Pots for the whole Time abovefaid ————	00	10	00			

carried over 129　15　00½

	l.	*s.*	*d.*
bro. over	129	15	00½

Item, Paid to *Richard Lincoln* Purveyor, for diverfe Neceffaries, by him bought and provided for and towards the melting and making of the Monies, *per* Bill — } 21 01 06

Item, Paid to him half a Year's Fee, after 20 *lb. per Ann.* as by his Receipt thereof ——— } 08 00 00

Item, Paid for the Moiety of the Officers Diets for *Octob.* 1647 } 07 14 09

Item, Paid to *Richard Sermon,* Collier, for Charcoal for the Melters, Monyers, Affayers, &c. — } 16 13 08

Item, Paid to *Edward Lote* for Sea Coals and Billets for the Moneyers, as *per* Bill ——— } 11 09 00

Item, Paid to *Thomas Hodgfkins,* Smith, for coining Irons, &c. *per* Bill ——— } 10 01 06

Item, Paid for Lofs arifing by breaking of the Monies for Trial of the Monies, *per* Bill —— } 03 05 07

Item, Paid to *John Reynolds, James Hoare,* and *Thomas Burghe,* Clerks, for half a Year to each — } 30 00 00

} 108 06 00

Sum total of the Difburfements is 238 01 00½

And fo this Accomptant hath paid more than received, by } 13 09 03

Before the *Norman* Conqueft the Kings of this Nation ordained and fet apart certain Monafteries for Mints, as the only Places for coining Money ; prefuming, that in fuch Places no Deceit or Corruption would be found. But this Ufage foon paffed away with our new Mafters ; for as early a See the clofe as the Reign of *Edward* I. we read [a] of a Mint Roll, 29 *Ed.* I. with thirty Furnaces in the Tower of *London* ; another with eight Furnaces at *Canterbury* ; another with four Furnaces at *Kingfton* upon *Hull* ; another with two Furnaces at *Newcaftle* upon *Tine* ; another with four Furnaces at *Briftol* ; and another with two Furnaces at *Exeter* ; all which is confirmed by the Infcription of diverfe ancient Coins,

Coins, which bear the Name of the Cities, &c. where they were coin'd.

Thus the State of the Mint continued fome times in one Place, and fometimes at another Place, according to the Pleafure or Will of the Prince, who fometimes was engaged by a Sum of Money to grant the Privilege of coining to fome Bifhop, Nobleman, or Corporation; till the Reign of Queen *Elizabeth*, who, in the Beginning of her Reign, began to remedy the Inconveniences that attended fuch promifcuous Coinage of the current Money, by reducing all the Mints to the Tower of *London*; fince which Time, Money has not been coined in *England*, any where elfe, except in the confufed Times of the Civil Wars, in King *Charles* I.'s Reign, when the King, being driven from his Capital, was obliged to erect new Mints at *York*, *Oxford*, and *Newark* upon *Trent*, the Places where he occafionally refided, when reduced to a Neceffity of coining Money to fupply his prefent Wants; and again, in the Year 1696, when King *William* III. having, for the Good of the Nation, called in the bad Money, erected Mints at *York*, *Exeter*, *Briftol*, and *Winchefter*; befides that in the Tower of *London*, to facilitate the Exchange of the faid Monies new coined to his Subjects.

The fame Power that has at all Times fixed and settled the Places for coining in this Nation, as it thought fit and convenient, has, at feveral times, altered and raifed the Price and Value of the Coins. Thus we read, that *Ofbright*, a *Saxon* King, 200 Years before the Conqueft by the *Normans*, ordained that an Ounce *Troy* of *Silver* fhould be divided into twenty Pieces or Pence; fo that an Ounce Troy of Silver was then of no more Value, than twenty Pence or five Groats.[a]

After the Conqueft, and not before the Days of King *Henry* III. it was enacted, that an *Englifh Penny*, called then a *Sterling*, round, and without any clipping, fhould weigh 32 Wheat Corns in the midft of the Ear; and that 20 of thefe Sterlings or Pence fhould make an *Ounce*.[b]

a See Sir *John Davys*'s Reports, fol. 23, b. and Sir *Matt. Hales*'s Treatife of Sher. Accounts, p. 9.
b See Statute *de Affifa Panis et Cerevifiæ*, fect. 3. *Anno* 51 *Hen.*III. and *Keb.* Stat. This fol. 10.

This was re-enacted in the 51ft of *Edward* I. with this Addition, that twelve fuch Ounces fhould make a Pound,[c] which was alfo agreed on, by the Statute of 12 *Henry* VII. concerning *Weights* and *Meafures:* So that a Pound Troy at that Time contained 240 Pence.[d]

c See the Ordi-
nance for Mea-
fures *eodem Anno,*
as alfo *Keble* fol.
68. and *Davys's*
ut fupra.
d See *Poulton's*
Pen. Stat. Title
*Weights and
Meafures,* fect. 2.
12 *Hen.*VII. c.5.
Keble fol. 329,
n. 4.

This, without Doubt, was a commendable Regulation; but it was foon found to be far from adjufting the true Value of the Metal, becaufe thefe Grains or Corns of Wheat fometimes weighed more, fometimes lefs, according to their Growth and Fulnefs; and were alfo fubject to the Influence of hot and moift Air; they were therefore reduced to *Artificial Grains,* cut out of thin Brafs, marked with 1, 2, 3, 4, &c. according to their Weight, or Number of Grains each of thofe thin Plates or Pieces of Brafs did weigh according to the King's Standard;[e] and then it was alfo ordained, that 24 of thefe Brafs Grains fhould go to one Penny weight. Where let me obferve, That as thefe *Brafs Grains* had, and ftill retain, the Name of *Grains,* from the *Grains of Wheat;* formerly ufed in Weight; fo the *Penny-weight,* or the *twentieth* Part of an *Ounce Troy,* ftill retains and keeps its old Name; tho' the Value of every *fuch* Penny-weight *now* is *three Pence,* which *then* was but a *Penny.* But,

e See *Hales's*
Treatife of Sher.
Accounts, c. 2.
p. 15,16,17,18.

King *Edward* III. obferving that foreign Nations raifed the Value of their Coins, ordained that the Ounce of Silver fhould be raifed alfo in *England* to 26 Pence; fo that a Pound Weight contained 312 Pence.[f] And for the fame Reafon King *Henry* VI. raifed it to 30 Pence; making a Pound to contain 360 Pence; each Penny being then worth *three Half-Pence.* King *Edward* IV. in the 5th Year of his Reign advanced it to forty Pence, or ten Groats the Ounce; which brought every Penny-weight to two Pence, and the Pound Weight to 480 of thefe Pence.[g]

f In 9 *Edw.*III.

g See Sir *Matt.
Hales,* as above,
and *Davys's* Re-
ports fol. 24, b.
Heyling's Eccl.
Reftaur. p. 135.
Leigh's Diatrib.
of Money, p.
59, 60.
Vaughan about
Coinage.

But when King *Henry* VIII. prepared for his Expedition to *Bulloyne,* he brought the Ounce of Silver to five and forty Pence, or, according to Sir *Richard Baker,* to four Shillings in Value or Currency; fo that the old Penny-weight was now worth

worth two Pence Farthing, and the Pound contained 540 of thefe Pence.   His Neceffities drove him alfo to coin bafe Money, mixed with Brafs; which continued current till the 5th *Edward* VI. when it was juftly cried down.[g]   This Debafement of the Sterling Money was the Reafon, why a Shilling after King *Henry*'s Death went but for Nine-Pence, and before they were cried down, only for Six-Pence; and the Groats in Proportion for three Pence and two Pence.

[g] See *Baker*'s Chron. fol. 295 & 312.

When Queen *Mary* found the Nation in this Diftrefs for Coin, fhe ordered the Groat, half Groat, and Penny, to be coined of Silver and Currency, as before her Father's Debafement thereof. Yet the Perfection of this good Work was not till Queen *Elizabeth*, fucceeding her Sifter on the Throne, embafed, and called in all Copper and bafe Money, in the fecond Year of her Reign by Proclamation.[h]   And her Intention being to deliver her Subjects from the Inconvenience and Damage, which they had laboured under for above 200 Years, by the bad Money of this Nation, fhe refolved to refine the Coin not according to the *legal*, but *natural* Eftimation of the Metal; and therefore ordered all the bafe Money to be marked, fome with a *Greyhound*, others with a *Portcullis*, and other fome with a *Lion, Harp, Rofe*, or *Flower de Lys*.   Then with all convenient Speed, fhe having received all this Money fo marked into her Majefty's Mint, repaid the Owners thereof fo much pure Sterling Silver, as the bafe Money was intrinfically worth in Silver, and no more; which memorable Action was more than King *Edward* VI. or Queen *Mary* durft attempt.*This Queen's next Care was to regulate the *Irifh* Coin; and fhe then raifed the Ounce of Silver to *fixty Pence* or *five Shillings*, which brought every *Penny-weight* to the old Standard of

[h] See *Camden*'s Remains, Title *Money*. *Speed*'s Chron. lib. 9. c. 24. *Stow*'s Annals § Edit. p. 1094.

B 3 *   *three*

---

* Queen *Elizabeth* alfo caufed all the foreign Coin, within her Realm of *England*, to be brought to the Mint, and new coined.   On which Occafion there was paid, 8,000, 10,000, 12,000, 16,000, 22,000 Pound of Silver Plate, and as much more in Piftoles and other Spanifh Gold, weekly, for the Space of half a Year.   See *Stow*'s Annals, p. 1096, and *Camden*, as before.

three Pence in Value, and thus it continues to this Day, to our Benefit, and a Memorial of that great Princefs's Wifdom.

Now from the Premifes it is eafy to collect, that the ancient current Silver Coin was the *Penny*, fo called from the *Saxon* Word *Penyg* or *Pennyg*,[i] and in *Latin*, as well as in Actions at Law, *Denarius*;[k] a Word ftill in Ufe among the *French* and *Italians*, who call all Money *Deniers*, or *Danari*. So the Penny Sterling was the Meafurement of all other our *Englifh* Silver Coins; thus the *Groat* contained four Pennies Sterling, and the *Half-Groat*, two Pennies Sterling; the *Shilling*, twelve Pennies Sterling; the *Half-Penny*, half a Sterling Penny; and the *Farthing*, the fourth Part of a Sterling Penny.

And now to conclude the whole, obferve, That our Accounts of Money have always been kept in *Pounds, Shillings, Pence,* and *Farthings*; and though the *Weight* of thefe have been frequently altered, and the *Finenefs* fometimes debafed, yet they have always borne the fame Proportion one to the other, as they do at this Time. There never was any fuch Piece coined as a *Pound*; but it was fo called as containing *twenty Shillings*, or 240 Penny-weights, or 12 Ounces Troy Weight. Nor was there fuch a Coin as a *Shilling*, till the 19 *Henry* VII. All which will better appear from the following Tables, Catalogues, and Faces of fuch Coins, as we have been able to find.

See *Coke* on *Littleton*, fol. 294, b.
k See *Davys's* Reports, fol. 24.

A TABLE

A Table expreſſing the true *Values* and
Weights of the *Silver Coin*, according
to the Account of the Mint in the
Tower of LONDON.

	s.	d.	dwt.	grs.	Mites	Droits	Perits	Blanks
Pieces of	5	0	19	8	10	8	—	—
	2	6	9	16	5	4	—	—
	1	0	3	20	18	1	10	—
	—	6	1	22	9	—	15	—
	—	2	—	15	9	16	5	—
	—	1	—	7	14	20	2	12
	—	½	—	3	17	10	1	6

Note, This Table is ſet forth in an Ordinance of Parliament,
paſſed 17 *July*, 1649.

A Table ſhewing, at one View, the
ſeveral Alterations before mentioned,
which have been made from Time to
Time, in the *Weight* and *Fineneſs* of
our *Silver Coins.*

Years	Money by Tale in a lb. wt. Troy		Fine Silver in a Pound Weight		Allay in a Pound Weight	
	s.	d.	oz.	dwt.	oz.	dwt.
From the Conqueſt to the Reign of *Edward* III.	20	—	11	2	—	18
20 *Edward* III.	22	6	11	2	—	18
27	25	—	11	2	—	18
9 *Henry* V.	30	—	11	2	—	18
1 *Henry* VI.	37	6	11	2	—	18
4	30	—	11	2	—	18
39	37	6	11	2	—	18
1 *Henry* VIII.	45	—	11	2	—	18
34	48	—	10	—	2	—
36	48	—	6	—	6	—
37	48	—	4	—	8	—
3 *Edward* VI.	72	—	6	—	6	—
5	72	—	3	—	9	—
6	60	—	11	1	—	19
1 *Mary* I.	60	—	11	—	1	—
2 *Elizabeth*	60	—	11	2	—	18
43	62	—	11	8	—	18

A

TABLE

OF THE

SILVER COINS

OF THE

Kings of *England*,

Which have been *Current* in the Kingdom of *England*; from the *Conquest*
to the Reign of King *George* I.

FROM the Conquest it does not appear that
the *Silver Coins* had any other Name or Value, than a *Penny* or *Sterling*, till 25 *Edward* III.
who coined

<table>
<tr><td></td><td>*Edward* III.</td><td>Pennies</td></tr>
<tr><td rowspan="4">* So called be-
cause they were
the *greatest* or
grossest Money
then in Use.</td><td></td><td>Grosses* or Groats</td></tr>
<tr><td></td><td>Half Groats</td></tr>
<tr><td>*Richard* II.</td><td>Groats</td></tr>
<tr><td></td><td>Half Groats</td></tr>
<tr><td></td><td></td><td>Sterlings</td></tr>
<tr><td></td><td></td><td>Half Sterlings</td></tr>
<tr><td></td><td>*Henry* IV.</td><td>The same. In this Reign it was
enacted, That a third Part of the
Bullion should be coined in *Half-
Pence* and *Farthings*</td></tr>
<tr><td></td><td>*Henry* V.</td><td>The same. After the Battle of *Agin-
court* he coined *Blanks*, or white
Pieces, rated *eight Pence*, or two
Groats</td></tr>
<tr><td></td><td>*Henry* VI.</td><td>The same. He was the first that
coined Brass Money in *Ireland*.</td></tr>
</table>

Edward

Edward IV. Groats
>   Three Pences, in the 18th Year of
>   his Reign
>   Two Pences
>   Pennies

Edward V. Groats
>   Pennies

Richard III. Groats.   *N. B.* This King's is the
>   moſt rare of all other Coins

Henry VII.   To the former Coins added the *Shil-*
>   *ling*, which weighed one third
>   more than ours at this Time.
>   [*Anno* 20.]

Henry VIII. Crown Pieces, one of which is now
>   preſerved by the Earl of *Pembroke*
>   Teſtoons or Shillings
>   Groats
>   Half Groats
>   Sterlings
>   Half Pence
>   Farthings

Edward VI. Crowns
>   Half Crowns
>   Teſtoons or Shillings
>   Six Pences
>   Groats
>   Three Pences

Q. *Mary* I. Shillings
>   Six Pences
>   Groats

Q. *Elizabeth* Crowns
>   Half Crowns
>   Shillings
>   Six Pences
>   Groats
>   Three Pences
>   Two Pences
>   Pennies

James I.   Crowns
>   Half Crowns
>   Shillings
>   Six Pences
>   Two Pences
>   Pence
>   Half Pence

Charles

Charles I. The fame. And after his Troubles began, he coined Groats, Three Pences, and other various Kinds of Money, which the Distraction of the Times and his urgent Necessities invented. *N. B.* This King's Coin appears with the most Variety.

After the 30th of *January*, 1648, the Parliament agreed upon a new Sort of Coin, by the Name of *Crowns, Half-Crowns, Shillings*, and *Six-Pences*, with this Inscription, *The Common-wealth of England*; on the Reverse, *God with us.* *Two Pences, Pennies, Half-Pennies*, with no Inscription, only the initial Figures. Their Sixpence in 1651, was the first milled Money in *England*. *Oliver*, usurping the Government, coined the first *English* Crown Piece milled, with an Inscription on the Rim, inscribed *Olivar, D. G. Ang. Scot. Hib.* &c. *PRO.* on the Reverse, *Pax Quæritur Bello*: a half Crown and a Shilling also milled

Charles II. Crowns, Half Crowns, Shillings, Six Pences, Groats, Three Pences, Two Pences, Pennies — *N. B.* In this Reign private Persons were indulged with a Liberty they had obtained in 1653 of coining their own Pennies, Half-Pence, and Farthings, till *An.*1672, when the King's Copper Half Pence and Farthings took Place.

James II. The fame. *N. B.* He coined Tin Farthings and Half Pence.

William III. and Mary II. The fame. He found the Coin so diminished, that Half a Crown would scarce weigh a Shilling, and so effectually cured and removed that Abuse, that we have enjoyed good Coin ever since.

Q. Anne The fame

A

A

TABLE

OF THE

GOLD COINS.

OF THE

Kings of *England.*

Edward III. Noble
           Half Noble
           Quarter Noble. *N. B.* His Son Prince
                Edward coined Gold in *Aquitaine*
Richard II. The fame
Henry IV. The fame
Henry V.   Noble
           Half Noble
           Quarter Noble
           Salute [coined in *France*]
Henry IV. Noble
           Half Noble
           Quarter Noble
           Salute
           Half Salute. Thefe two laft were
               coined in *France*
Edward IV. Spurr Royal
           Half Spurr Royal
           Angel. This firft coined *Anno* 1465
           Half Angel
Richard III. Spurr Royal
           Angel
           Half Angel
Henry VII. Quadruple Rofe Noble
           Double Rofe Noble
           Spur Royal
           Angel
           Half Angel

Henry

Henry VIII. Double Rofe Noble
Spurr Royal
Sovereign, *(viz.) on his Throne*
Half Sovereign
George Noble
Angel
Half Angel
Quarter Angel
Crown with the Rofe, *H. R.*
Half Crown with the Rofe, *H. R.*
Crowns with *H.I. H.K.* and *H.A.* on
the Reverfe
*Edward*VI. Double Rofe Noble
Spurr Royal
Sovereign
Half Sovereign
Angel
Half Angel
Broad Piece with his Demi Effigies in
Armour
Half Broad Piece, ditto
Ten Shilling Piece with the Crown on
his Head
Half 10*s.* or Crown Piece, ditto
Quarter or Half Crown, ditto
Ten Shilling Piece, exhibiting him
bare-headed
Half 10*s.* or Crown, ditto
Quarter or Half Crown, ditto
Ten Shilling Piece, bare-headed, with
the Rofe inftead of the King's Arms
on the Reverfe.
Q. *Mary* I. Double Rofe Noble, 1553
Spurr Royal, 1553
Angel
Half Angel
Philip and ⎱ Angel
Mary I. ⎰ Half Angel
Crown, with *Mundi falus unica*
Q.*Elizabeth* Double Rofe Noble
Spurr Royal
Broad Piece
Half Broad Piece
Quarter Broad Piece
Half Quarter Broad Piece

Q. *Elizabeth*

Q. *Elizabeth* Half Broad Piece and Quarter neatly
wrought and milled. [Thofe grained
or indented on the Edges are rare.]
Angel
Half Angel
Quarter Angel

James I.   Double Rofe Noble
Spurr Royal
Sovereign or 30 s. Piece
Half Sovereign or 15 s. Piece
Scepter and Globe Piece, or 28 s. with
  Rex Angliæ & Scotiæ
Half of the fame
Scepter and Globe, or 25 s. Piece
Half Scepter, or 12 s. 6 d. Piece
Quarter of the fame
Half Quarter of the fame
Broad or 20 s. Piece, Head Laureated
Half or 10 s. Piece, Head Laureated
Quarter of the fame, or 5 s. Piece
Angel
Half Angel
Crown, called the Thiftle Crown

Charles I.   Spurr Royal
Broad, or 20 s. Piece
Half or 10 s. Piece
Quarter or 5 s. Piece.   Of thefe there
  are three particular Sorts, *viz.*
  with the Ruff plain, and fmart Ruff
  with the Garter Robes, and Broad
  band, of 20 s. 10 s. and 5 s.
Angel.   In his Troubles he coined
  3 *l.* or 3 Broads with the Sword
  and Laurel Branch; and alfo 20 s.
  or fingle Broads and Half Broads,
  or 10 s. Pieces of the fame.   In
  Scotland he coined a Broad Piece
  with the Scepter and Globe of 25 s.

Commonwealth Broad or 20 s. Pieces
Half
Quarter

Oliver   Twenty Shilling Piece milled, excel-
  lently done by *Symonds,* 1656.

Charles II.

Charles II.   Broad or 20 s. Piece with the small
              Crown.   The Mint Mark
              Ten Shilling
              Five Shilling Piece, ditto
              Broad Piece milled of 20 s. by *Symonds,*
              An. 1662
              Half and
              Quarter of the same.   He was the
              first that coined 5 Pound or 5 Gui-
              nea Pieces, Double or 2 Guineas
              Guineas, and Half Guineas milled
James II.   Five Guineas
              Double Guines
              Guineas
              Half Guineas
William III. ⎱
and *Mary*II. ⎰ The same
Q. *Anne*   The same

*In the Prefs, and is propofed to be publifhed the 25th of March,*1745. *Beautifully printed in Two Volumes in Folio,*

A

COLLECTION

O F

Voyages *and* Travels:

Confifting of

Authentic Writers in our own Tongue, which have not been collected before in *Englifh*; or, have only appeared in Epitome in other Collections:

And continued with

Others of Note that have publifhed Hiftories, Voyages, Travels, Journals, or Difcoveries, in the *Englifh*, *Latin*, *French*, *Italian*, *Spanifh*, *Portuguefe*, *Dutch* or *German* Tongues:

R E L A T I N G

To any Part of the Continent of *Afia*, *Africa*, *America*, *Europe*, or the Iflands thereof, from the earlieft Account, to the prefent Time :

D I G E S T E D

According to the Parts of the World to which they relate; with Hiftorical Introductions to each Account, containing the Lives of their Authors, or what elfe can be difcovered and is thought neceffary to inform and entertain the Reader.

W I T H

Great Variety of ufeful Charts and Maps, and Cuts of the greateft Curiofities to be found recorded in the Courfe of this Work, engraven on Copper Plates.

C O M P I L E D

From the curious and valuable LIBRARY

Of the late

E A R L O F O X F O R D.

Interfperfed and Illuftrated

With fome general Account of the Difcovery of each Country, or an Abftract of its Hiftories, a Differtation on its Government, Religion, &c. and with many ufeful Notes, Original Letters, Papers, Letters Patents. Charters, Acts of Parliament, &c. proper to explain many obfcure Paffages, which are too often found in other Collections of this Kind.

London, *Oct.* 8, 1744.

PROPOSALS

For ENGRAVING by SUBSCRIPTION,

TWENTY

OF THE

Capital Antique Statues

IN

ROME AND *FLORENCE*.

Done in a very Large Size,

From the Drawings of Mr. *Richd. Dalton.*

CONDITIONS.

I. THEY will be ENGRAVED by the beſt Hands that can be procured either at Home or Abroad.

II. The firſt Print, Engraved by *Wagner* at *Venice,* will be deliver'd at the Time of Subſcribing, and the Reſt as faſt as they can be Engraved, the Drawings being all Finiſhed.

III. They will be printed on the beſt Imperial Paper.

IV. The Price to *Subſcribers* will be Fifty Shillings: Twenty to be paid at the Time of Subſcribing, and the Remainder at Eighteen-pence each Print, as they are deliver'd.

N.B. *Whoever Subſcribes for Six ſhall have a Seventh* gratis.

A SPECIMEN of the Work, being the Dying GLADIATOR, may be ſeen at the following Places, where *Subſcriptions* are taken in, *viz.*

R. DODSLEY, at *Tully's-Head* in *Pall-Mall*; T. OSBORNE, *Gray's-Inn*; G. HAWKINS, at *Milton's-Head, Temple-bar*; J. BRACKSTONE, at the *Globe* in *Cornhill*; and S. SIMPSON, Printſeller, in *Maiden-Lane.*

Plate. VII.

English Gold Coins.

Edward. III half Penny.
of Gold

Half Noble.
C. 3.

Henry. V. Noble.

Richard. II half Penny of Gold.

Henry. VI. Rose Noble or Ryal.

Henry. V. Salute.

Henry. VI. Angel.

Plate .VIII.

Henry.VII. Sovereign.

Crown of Gold Hen.VIII.

Henry.VIII. Angel.

Henry.VIII. Sovereign.

Edward.VI. Noble.

Henry.VIII. Noble.

Plate IX.

2. Elizabeth's Rose Royal.

2. Eliza. Sovereign.

2. Eliz: half Sovereign.

2. Eliz. Angel.

2. Eliz: Spur Royal.

Plate X.

James. I. Rose Royal of 33 Shil·

James. I. Rose Royal of 30 Shil:

K. James, I. Unite·   *James. I. Laurel.*   *James. I. Spur Royal,*

Val. 22s.   *Val.* 20s.

Plate XI.

K. James I, Spur Royal.

K. James I. Angel.

Val. XI. Shil.

James I double Brit. Crown.

James, I, Laurel.

James I. Angel.

Val. X. Shil.

Charles I. Rose Royal.

Ja: I. Brit Crown.

James I, V. S. Laurel.

Plate XII.

K. Char. I. Unite

Char. I. Spur Royal

K. Char. I. half Unite

Charles I. Angel.

The XXI. Piece of ye Commonwealth

K. Char. I. Crown.

X. s. Piece.

V. s. Piece.

Plate XII.

K. Char: I. Unite

Char: I. Spur Royal

K. Char: I. half Unite

Charles I. Angel.

The XX Piece of ye Commonwealth

K. Char: I. Crown.

X. s. Piece.

V. s. Piece.